POWER
MOMENTS

Positive Motivation
and
Powerful Inspiration

Power for Living

The Radio Ministry of Pastor Mike Cramer

New Life Baptist Church
11593 McKinley Hwy. E. / Osceola, IN 46561
(574) 674-2868 • pflmike@aol.com

15 Minutes of Motivation & Inspiration Every Sunday

7:15 a.m.	8:15 a.m.	9:00 a.m.
WSBT 960AM	WBRI 1500AM	WFRN 1270AM
South Bend, IN	Indianapolis, IN	Elkhart, IN

Michael A. Cramer

Produced by JM Press, Brentwood, TN 37027-1911

ISBN: 0-9717532-0-2

DEDICATION

I dedicate this book to my beautiful wife, Cindi. I thank God for her faithful support and loving influence in my life and ministry. She is my greatest encourager and my closest friend. Together we have experienced our greatest joy and most important ministry through being involved in the lives of our four outstanding children: Michael, Joseph, Jacob, and Hannah.

CONTENTS

INTRODUCTION

This book is designed to increase your faith in God and ignite your vision for success in life. The fifty-two chapters were created to offer you positive motivation and powerful inspiration on a weekly basis. Each chapter contains an inspirational story to lift your spirit and a scriptural principle to build on a foundation for success. You may choose to read the chapters in consecutive order, but it is not necessary to do so. Chapter 27 was written to increase your patriotic spirit and Chapter 51 is provided to help celebrate the true meaning of Christmas. My goal is that every chapter will encourage you in your journey of faith and inspire your passion for success.

The purpose of the Power for Living Ministry is to communicate a positive Christian message and empower people to achieve success through the motivational and inspirational teaching of sacred truth. Therefore, I trust that the pages of this book will bring "Power Moments" to your life.

—Michael A. Cramer

CHAPTER 1

EVERY OBSTACLE IS
A POTENTIAL OPPORTUNITY

The Scripture says in Romans 8:28:

And we know that all things work together for good to those who love God, to those who are the called according to His purpose.

Believing this positive promise from the Word of God will certainly help us view every obstacle as a potential opportunity.

The Bible is filled with examples of people who faced great challenges and experienced tremendous victories. David certainly faced an obstacle when he went against the enormous giant named Goliath. However, his faith turned the obstacle into an opportunity to experience the power of God. David proved that giants fall when faith overcomes fear.

Daniel faced an obstacle when he was thrown into the Lion's Den. Once again, it was an opportunity to experience the power of God. Daniel propped his head on the lions, like they were pillows, and slept like a baby as God closed their mouths.

The three Hebrew children, Shadrach, Meshack and Abednego, certainly faced an obstacle as they were thrown into the fiery furnace. Everyone thought their "goose was cooked." However, they could "stand the heat" as God kept them calm, cool and collected.

We could go on and on. That is why Romans 8:31 says:

What then shall we say to these things? If God is for us, who can be against us?

Let's face it, we all experience obstacles, don't we? Perhaps it's a new job, peer pressure at school, a strained relationship with an old friend, or maybe a problem in the home. We can become discouraged when we focus our attention simply on the obstacle. However, learning to look through the eye of faith will help us see our obstacle as a potential opportunity to experience the power of God.

My friend, many people who have achieved greatness began by overcoming tremendous obstacles. One example is former Yankee great, Joe DiMaggio. In fact, his obstacle actually became his opportunity to achieve incredible success.

His obstacle was a weak stomach, which kept him from the family fishing business. His dad was a fisherman by trade and was proud of the occupation that had been in the family for generations. Joe's dad worked hard at expanding the business and dreamed of his son carrying on the family tradition.

However, the smell of fish literally made Joe sick to his stomach. This kept him from working in the fishing business. His dad told him he was lazy and "good for nothing." This caused Joe to try even harder to overcome his obstacle of a weak stomach. But try as he did, he just could not take the smell of the fish. Joe even tried to work in the business by repairing the nets. However, the strong smell of fish was deeply embedded into the nets. Consequently, his queasy stomach could not even handle repairing them.

Finally, with deep agony in his soul, Joe quit the fishing business. He was painfully aware that he was an enormous disappointment to his father. Eventually, driven by despair, Joe decided to dedicate himself to baseball. He truly loved the game and seemed very gifted at it. In fact, in spite of his dad's rejection, he discovered his true talent was obviously playing the game of baseball. Eventually, the New York Yankees became very glad that Joe DiMaggio had a weak stomach and was unfit for the family fishing business.

As you know, Joe DiMaggio became one of the greatest baseball players of all time. He set the major league record of hitting safely in 56 consecutive games. Three times he was the American League MVP. Twice he was the American League Batting Champion. Not to mention, he won nine World Series Championships while playing for the New York Yankees. As you remember this "hall of famer," keep in mind that his obstacle led to his opportunity to succeed.

Just think, if he would not have had the obstacle of a weak stomach, he may have never discovered his true talent. By the way, I'll bet his father eventually changed his mind about calling Joe a "good for nothing."

Friend, with the help of God, we can all learn to view our obstacles as potential opportunities. Because of the resurrection of Jesus Christ, we can personally experience the promise that "with God all things are possible." In fact, the greatest obstacle that we all face is our need to be reconciled to God. However, this obstacle can be turned into a great opportunity to learn of the incredible love of God found in Jesus Christ our Lord. The Bible says in Romans 5:8:

But God demonstrates His own love toward us, in that while we were still sinners, Christ died for us.

Yes, God loves you today. He saw enough value in your life that He gave His Son in order for you to have the opportunity to experience a personal relationship with God. Simply affirm your faith in the Lord by telling God you believe Jesus died and rose again for you.

Remember my friend; "God causes all things to work together for good to those who love God." Therefore, do not panic the next time your "back is against the wall." Simply take the opportunity to trust God to bring down your "walls of obstacles" just as He tore down the "Walls of Jericho." After all, the obstacle that initially makes you "sick to your stomach" could be what God uses to bring the "sweet smell of success." Yes, keep your eyes on Christ and He will help you turn every obstacle into a potential opportunity.

CHAPTER 2

CONFIDENCE MEANS:
BELIEVE IT AND YOU CAN ACHIEVE IT

Confidence is a very important character quality of a true champion. Confidence is that inner quality that quietly commands the respect of others. Confidence is a funny thing. If you don't have it, no one can give it to you. However, if you have inner confidence then no one can take it from you. Yes, confidence means: believe it and you can achieve it.

I believe the Christian ought to be a confident person. Jesus said in Matthew 19:26: "with God all things are possible." Yes, learning to look at a situation through the lens of scripture and the eye of faith will ignite your confidence.

First, you will know you are on the winning team. After all, I Corinthians. 15:57 says:

But thanks be to God, who gives us the victory through our Lord Jesus Christ.

That's right my friend, the resurrection of Jesus Christ settled the score once and for all. The enemy has been defeated and the believer is victorious. The believer can rest assured that Jesus has conquered sin, death, and hell itself. Jesus died and rose again to provide us forgiveness of sins, a home in heaven, victory over the enemy, and the resurrection power of Christ in our life on Earth.

The Christian should have embedded in their mind the phrase: "With God all things are possible." The believer can be an agent of positive change in our negative world. The Christian has the perspective to see a situation not simply as it is, but how it could be with the help of the Lord. The Christian has the power of God within them to see the potential around them.

The believer can live a life that has the trademark of confidence in God. After all, we know of His powerful workings in the past and we believe God is still at work today. Hebrews 13:8 says:

Jesus Christ is the same yesterday, today and forever.

The positive minded Christian is not afraid to accept a great challenge. Their inner confidence is based on a personal relationship with the Lord. They welcome the opportunity to overcome an enormous obstacle. They have learned to: attempt great things for God; accept great things from God, and achieve great things with God.

The words of Jesus: "With God all things are possible," are not idle chatter to the positive Christian. They are words that inspire them to: "Believe it and you can achieve it!" They know that mountains are not something to walk away from. They choose to climb over it, walk around it, tunnel through it, or simply turn it into a gold mine.

Confident people look for the potential in any situation. Their focus is on the possibility not the problem. The former great quarterback Johnny Unitas said this about confidence: " There is a difference between conceit and confidence. Conceit is bragging about yourself. Confidence means you believe you can get the job done. I have always believed I could get the job done."

My friend, I like Johnny Unitas' view of confidence. Why not develop the inner quality of confidence that believes you can get the job done? Especially for the believer in the Lord.

After all, the believer has the power of God upon their life. Joshua 1:9 says:

Have I not commanded you? Be strong and of good courage; do not be afraid, nor be dismayed, for the Lord your God is with you wherever you go.

That's right my friend. The Christian has the great promise of living with the presence of the Lord. That will boost your confidence. It can change your outlook as you develop your up look.

It is like the Biblical story of David and Goliath. The negative people said that Goliath was too big to hit. It seems that fear and negativity go hand in hand. However, David took one look at Goliath and said he was too big to miss! Yes, confidence and a positive faith in God go hand in hand, as well.

The Apostle Paul said in Philippians 4:13:

I can do all things through Christ who strengthens me.

Yes, a person with a positive attitude and personal faith in God says to himself: "I believe and I can achieve." The inner drive is pounding in their soul and pushes them to new goals. Today's success is simply yesterday's impossibilities. Therefore, they know that even greater things can be in store for tomorrow.

My friend, many successful people have learned to overcome the odds. Often times they had to believe in themselves when others did not. Sometimes, they were the only person who knew their success was within reach.

For example, George Dantzig made mathematical history a number of years ago. He solved the two "unsolvable problems." In one week, he achieved what Albert Einstein was unable to accomplish in his entire lifetime.

It seems that Dantzig was taking his final exam as a math major at the University of California at Berkley. He was highly motivated to do his best. After all, the school had offered a math-teaching job to the student with the highest score on the final exam. The Great Depression had caused "tough times" all across the nation and jobs were extremely scarce. Therefore, he studied with fierce determination because he desperately needed a job.

In fact, he studied so long and hard that he arrived late for class on the day of the final exam. Therefore, he was unaware of the instructions the professor had given for the exam. The professor handed out a test with eight problems. That was the actual exam. Then the professor put two problems on the board and told the students to tinker around for the rest of their lives on them. The professor explained that Einstein himself was unable to solve the two impossible mathematical problems.

However, since Dantzig had arrived late for class, he did not realize that the two problems on the board were not part of the exam. Consequently, once he finished the first eight problems, he then began working on the two remaining problems on the board. Naturally, he struggled with the problems so he requested more time to finish the exam.

Therefore, the professor gave him a few more days to finish. George worked day and night for the next few days on the difficult problems. He needed the job and he was bound and determined to solve the questions. He believed in his ability and was confident that he could find the correct answers to the problems.

Finally, he made a startling break through and solved the first problem. This inspired his confidence to solve the remaining problem. Sure enough, he achieved his goal. However, he did not realize that he had made mathematical history!

The professor was shocked when Dantzig turned in the exam with all of the problems solved. He explained to Dantzig that the two problems on the board were never meant to be a part of the exam. The professor was wild with excitement as he told George Dantzig of his mathematical achievement! He also guaranteed that Dantzig would get the math-teaching job.

Think about it. George Dantzig did not set a limit on himself because he did not know the problems were considered "unsolvable." He accomplished the "impossible" because his confidence helped him "believe it and achieve it." He left his mark on this world and achieved greatness because he set a goal based on his own ability. Keep in mind that he did not have the help of a computer. He did it the old fashioned way. He stretched his mind and he rose to meet the challenge.

My friend, you can accomplish great things as well. Jesus said in Mark 9:23, "All things are possible to him who believes." Keep your confidence in the Lord and set goals that will make you stretch for success. Always remember, confidence means: believe it and you can achieve it.

Chapter 3

Encouragement Means:
Look for the Good and You Will Find It

I want to consider the all-important subject of encouragement. Let's face it, everyone needs a "pat on the back" or an occasional "shot in the arm." Encouragement simply stated is: "Look for the Good and you will find it."

Proverbs 12:25 says:

Anxiety in the heart of man causes depression, but a good word makes it glad.

The word "worry" or "anxiety" is an interesting word picture in the Bible. It paints the picture of a piece of clothing that is coming apart at the seams. It also gives the idea of two animals tied to something and pulling in two different directions.

The picture is so clear. Anxiety makes a person feel like they are being torn apart. They may feel like their emotional health is unraveling. It is an emotional feeling of "coming apart at the seams." It causes great depression to the inner spirit. It can be a feeling of hopelessness and helplessness. Worry is so damaging to the mental frame of mind.

Worry causes our problems to appear larger than they truly are. Anxiety will cause us to build "mental monsters" in our mind. We will build mental mountains out of mole hills. Everything begins to bring us down as we worry and build our problems up.

Here is the amazing fact. God says that a simple kind word can cheer up someone. A good word can encourage someone to "snap out" of their poor mental frame of mind. A good word will inspire someone with courage and hope. A positive outlook will be born from a positive word of affirmation.

My friend, it has been said that everyone carries two buckets. A bucket of gas and a bucket of water. We can pour the bucket of gas or water on what we choose.

For example, the negative person will pour their bucket of gas on a spark of negativity. This will cause the negative attitudes to spread like wild fire. They will then turn around and pour their bucket of water on the positive spark. This will douse out any hope of encouragement.

However, the positive person will pour their bucket of gas on the spark of hope and inspiration. This will cause people to look forward to a bright future. They will truly believe that the best is yet to come. The positive person will also pour their bucket of water on the negative spark. They will quickly put out the spirit of discouragement and despair. Positive people influence others in an encouraging way.

Proverbs 18:21 says:

Death and life are in the power of the tongue, and those who love it will eat its fruit.

Bottom line, positive people have learned to look for the good and they always find it. When life hands them a lemon, they just make lemonade. They bring out the best in any situation. Most importantly, positive people will always bring out the best in other people.

Trust me on one thing. When you are around an encouraging person, you will know it. By the way, when you are an encouraging person, others will enjoy being around you as well.

Yes, "death and life are in the power of the tongue, and those who love it will eat of its fruit." I guess we have to decide what type of "fruit" we want our words to be. Do we want our words to be like "spoiled fruit" that makes someone sick; or do we choose to make our words: "good fruit" that brings emotional health to others.

My friend, that is why it is so important to guard your heart. After all, Jesus said that, "out of the abundance of the heart the mouth speaks." Yes, our words simply indicate what our mind and heart has been focused on.

That is exactly why the Word of God instructs us to feed our mind with positive thoughts. Philippians 4:8 says:

Finally, brethren, whatever things are true, whatever things are noble, whatever things are just, whatever things are pure, whatever things are lovely, whatever things are of good report, if there is any virtue and if there is anything praiseworthy-meditate on these things.

Yes, put good things into your mind. Feast your thoughts on the positive aspects of life. Focus on the goodness of the Lord. Keep your attitude positive and your words will be pleasant. That is so much better than the poisonous infection of a negative attitude. People will benefit as you "look for the good and find it."

You know, a number of years ago I studied for my Masters degree in Ministry at the Moody Bible Institute in Chicago. I will never forget my first class. It was entitled "excellence in leadership" and was taught by Dr. Thomas Stevenin.

The first day of class we introduced ourselves and where we were serving in ministry. We were enrolled in a modular style program so there were people from all over the country in the class. We would go to Chicago for a week-long class of intensive training and then complete the additional class work by correspondence.

There were about 45 pastors in the classroom from ministries throughout the United States. Each one of us gave our name and the church where we were serving as pastor. Dr Stevenin just smiled and thanked us for introducing ourselves.

Then he began teaching the class on leadership. Dr Stevenin was a Christian businessman and senior partner in a prestigious consulting firm. The leadership principles he taught were outstanding.

However, his teaching method and delivery style were a little dry. Then he did something that grabbed my attention for the rest of the week. About an hour into the first class session, he smiled and said: "Let me make sure I've become acquainted with everyone." The next thing he did was truly amazing. Dr Stevenin named all 45 pastors by first and last name and correctly stated where each one was serving in ministry.

Believe me, this man now had my complete and undivided attention. It was a remarkable display of brilliance and concentration. After all, he had just met us for the first time only an hour before.

However, his own personal story was even more incredible. Later in the week he was emphasizing the importance of encouragement. He pointed out how affirming love and encouragement would bring out the best in others.

Then he told us how his fourth grade teacher, Nettie, had influenced him. At that time, he could not even spell his own name. People called him Tommy in those days, but he always spelled it "YMOT." The school had diagnosed him as severely retarded and requested that he be removed. However, his parents insisted that he be placed in the school. No teacher wanted him except Nettie. She loved teaching and most importantly, she loved her students.

One day Nettie asked little Tommy to stay after class. She looked at Tommy and told him that he had a wonderful mind. Tommy was shocked to say the least. After all, he was in the fourth grade and could not even write his own name. Then Nettie made an amazing agreement with Tommy. She told him she would give him an "A" in all of his subjects once he learned to write his name correctly six times in a row.

Tommy worked and worked. Nettie invited him over on Saturdays to her house. She gave him all kinds of encouragement and special attention. Finally, he learned to spell his name. Nettie came through and gave him an "A" in every subject.

The next year he was shocked on the first day of school. Standing in his fifth grade classroom was Miss Nettie. It was the only time in 40 years she moved up and taught the fifth grade. Once again, Nettie worked and worked with little Tommy.

Tommy went on to become a model student. Later on he was diagnosed as being dyslexic. He learned how to correct the problem and eventually earned a Ph.D.

Dr Stevenin says in his book, "People Power", that he owes all of his success to Nettie Weirdenmann, his fourth and fifth grade teacher. She knew the value of encouraging him and truly brought out the best in him.

Dr Stevenin has now gone home to be with the Lord but his influence lives on. The instruction I received from him concerning encouragement has made me a better pastor and leader. I am grateful for the influence of his teaching on my life.

My friend, be a positive person and encourage someone today. Remember, encouragement means: look for the good and you will find it.

CHAPTER 4

WINNERS GIVE EXTRA EFFORT—NOT EXCUSES

Winners in life are people with that immeasurable quality called "heart." This gives them the power to persevere in the midst of any difficult challenge. The person who gets knocked down 100 times and gets up 99 times is incredible. However, the person who gets up 100 times is invincible. Winners give extra effort, not excuses.

Galatians 6:9 says:

And let us not grow weary while doing good, for in due season we shall reap if we do not lose heart.

Yes, winners in life "keep on keeping on." When they face a challenge, they simply refuse to quit. They live by the principle that, "When the going gets tough, the tough get going." The word quit is removed from their vocabulary. Vince Lombardi said, "It is not whether you get knocked down, it is whether you get up."

Winners in life spell talent: w-o-r-k. They recognize that success has no shortcuts. Proverbs 13:4 says:

The soul of a lazy man desires, and has nothing; but the soul of the diligent shall be made rich.

Yes, hard work and a determination to succeed go hand in hand. The true winner achieves his success the "old-fashioned way"—he works for it.

Winners will develop a positive attitude. Luke 1:37 says: "For with God nothing will be impossible." Yes, achievement always begins with your attitude.

I'm reminded of the success story of Rocky Blier. He is a vintage example of hard work with total heart. He played college football at Notre Dame and had a tremendous desire to play pro football. In 1968, Rocky Blier was the Pittsburgh Steelers last pick of the eighteenth round. However, he was also drafted by the Army and sent to Vietnam.

While bravely serving his country, Rocky was tragically wounded in battle. The bottom of his right foot was ripped open with a grenade. His right leg was shredded by shrapnel and his left thigh was hit by gunfire. Rocky Blier was listed as 40% disabled.

The doctors told him his football career was over. However, Rocky refused to give up his dream of playing in the NFL. He was determined to persevere. He chose to spell talent: w-o-r-k. He decided to give extra effort not excuses.

Therefore, Rocky had a special shoe made for his right foot and began his uphill climb for success. He rose early and ran every day. He lifted weights in the afternoon and ran again in the evening. It was a grueling workout as he pushed himself beyond human limitations.

In 1970, he showed up to the Pittsburgh Steelers training camp. Rocky limped badly, but refused to quit. He was an inspiration to everyone on the team. However, he was the last player cut that year. He tried out again the next season and ripped his hamstring muscle in the leg that had been shot. The doctors and coaches saved their breath in even trying to suggest he quit.

Finally, in 1972, Rocky made the special teams unit. To everyone's surprise, he was actually running faster than before his injury. By 1974, he was in the starting backfield with Franco Harris. In 1976, Rocky Blier rushed for over 1000 yards.

His refusal to quit paved the way for incredible success. Rocky Blier was a key player for the Pittsburgh Steelers during the 1970's, as they dominated pro football and won four Super Bowl championships!

My friend, winners give extra effort not excuses. Most people would have given up and "thrown in the towel." However, the difference between the "average" and the "great" is that simple word called "perseverance." The ability to refuse to allow a negative situation to destroy their positive spirit. The courage to face a challenge with faith and not shrink back in fear.

Psalm 27:13-14 says:

I would have lost heart, unless I had believed that I would see the goodness of the Lord in the land of the living. Wait on the Lord; Be of good courage, And He shall strengthen your heart; Wait, I say, on the Lord!

Yes, the person of positive faith will believe in a powerful God who will uphold them in difficult times. God will give you the courage to face the future and the faith to believe - "the best is yet to come."

You know, one of my favorite hobbies is coaching. I love it. I have coached soccer, basketball, little league, flag football, and elementary tackle football, known as rocket football. The biggest reason I love coaching is the simple fact that it is a great opportunity to teach about life.

I love to challenge young athletes to dig deep and determine to work hard. I enjoy teaching eager minds how hard work and discipline pay off in athletics and also pay off in life. Oh, we have fun for sure, but we also learn how to discipline ourselves even when it is not fun. The end result is the reward of a solid performance and doing our best. In my opinion, it is also a good way to teach self-esteem through hard work and achievement. It is exciting to instill confidence in the athletes and turn them loose as they learn to believe in themselves.

I believe that winners in life are people who develop a winning mindset and refuse to make excuses. The easy road in life is paved with excuses of losers. However, the hard road that leads to success is led by people who give extra effort not excuses.

One of the highlights of these various coaching experiences came a few years ago while coaching rocket football. We took a group of fifth and sixth grade boys and entered them in a tackle football league. None of the boys on the team had any previous experience. However, we would be playing other teams that had been together for three to four years. Therefore, we knew we would have to give extra effort to even compete with the more experienced teams.

Our motto for the season was - "Winners give extra effort not excuses." We practiced on the fundamentals of the game in order to learn the basics of football. Most importantly, we took every opportunity to relate football to the game of life.

During each practice we would have a "chalk talk" on character. Our goal was to use the football experience as a vehicle to develop championship character. The parents loved it! They would smile and nod their heads with approval and affirmation as we taught winning values and life skills.

The end result was the fact that the wins took care of themselves. In fact, the team went undefeated! The culmination of our efforts came in the final drive of the championship game. Trailing late in the fourth quarter, the boys drove the ball 87 yards in the final two minutes and twenty-two seconds of the game. They scored the game-winning touchdown with only twenty-three seconds left on the clock.

We were ecstatic! After the game, all of the parents and fans gathered around the championship team. We reviewed our character principle that: "Winners give extra effort not excuses." It was a tremendous accomplishment and a lesson on life the boys will never forget. My son, Jacob, was on the team and we still cherish the memory.

We honored the team at New Life Baptist Church, where I serve as pastor. Over 700 people gave a thunderous applause for the championship character displayed in their tremendous achievement. Parents and grandparents looked on with pride as they treasured the memory.

My friend, do you face a challenge today?   Look to God through the eye of faith. He will listen to your prayer for help. God says in Jeremiah 33:3:

Call to Me, and I will answer you, and show you great and mighty things, which you do not know.

That's right, God is ready to listen and willing to answer your prayer. God will do things in your life that go beyond your imagination. Therefore, set a goal and let nothing detract you from it. After all, God says in His Word, "we shall reap if we do not lose heart." God will help you be a winner in the game of life and empower you with a spirit of perseverance. Remember, winners give extra effort not excuses.

CHAPTER 5

IF YOU WANT TO SOAR LIKE AN EAGLE, YOU CANNOT THINK LIKE A CHICKEN

So much of success or failure is due to our mental frame of mind. People who think like a winner become a winner. They surround themselves with people who have a hunger to succeed. After all, success breeds success.

Confidence grows in a positive atmosphere where people are out to pursue their dreams. Goals are set and plans are made. Energy and enthusiasm flourish in the fertile ground of encouragement.

Yes, if you want to soar like an eagle, you cannot think like a chicken. My friend, a positive mental attitude is a Biblical principle as well. In the New Testament book of Philippians Chapter 4 and verse 8 the Bible says-

Finally, brethren, whatever things are true, whatever things are noble, whatever things are just, whatever things are pure, whatever things are lovely, whatever things are of good report, if there is any virtue and if there is anything praiseworthy-meditate on these things.

Yes, God wants us to think on good things. A positive outlook is a spiritual outlook. It is simply the right way to think. A positive outlook will help you on the road to success.

The Scripture says in Proverbs 23:7 that as a man thinks in his heart, so is he. In other words, we are what we think. Our thought process will directly affect our inner spirit and our will to achieve. A positive outlook will produce positive results.

However, the opposite can be true as well. A negative outlook will pull you down. The "Nay Sayers" become the dream killers.

Good ideas get shot down before they can be developed into great plans. Mediocrity becomes the standard. Fear of failure keeps people from tasting the sweetness of success. The idea gets spoiled in the garbage pail of negativity. People simply do not soar like an eagle when everyone thinks like a chicken.

The legendary story is told of a farmer who came upon an eagle's egg. Somehow the eagle's egg had wound up on the ground of the barnyard. The farmer picked up the eagle's egg and mistakenly thought it was another chicken's egg. Consequently, he carried the egg to the chicken coop and placed it with some eggs in a hen's nest.

The mother hen covered the eagle's egg with her wings. She protected the egg just like all the others. The eagle's egg was able to go through its incubation period safe and secure.

In time, all of the eggs hatched. There was this little baby eagle among the little chickens. However, the eagle just assumed it was a chicken. As the eagle grew, it mimicked the actions of the chickens. It walked like the chickens and acted like the chickens. This poor eagle learned to cluck and scratch like a chicken.

Because the eagle thought and acted like a chicken, it was not learning to soar like an eagle. It wandered around the barnyard flapping its wings like a chicken. This pitiful eagle would only fly a few feet in the air. It did not realize it was capable of soaring high in the sky. The eagle ate like a chicken, walked like a chicken, talked like a chicken, because it believed it was a chicken. After all, it had been surrounded by chickens all its life. The eagle had absolutely no reason not to believe it was not a chicken.

One day the little eagle looked up in the sky and beheld a bird soaring in the air. This bird was flying higher than he had ever imagined possible. It was a majestic creature to behold.

The little eagle turned to the chickens and said, "I want to fly like that bird when I grow up. Look how it soars in those wide circles high above the ground." All the chickens laughed and said, "Don't be crazy, that is an eagle and you are only a chicken. You could never fly like that!"

However, the little eagle continued to study the bird soaring through the air. He decided to give it a try. Much to his amazement, he began rising more than a few feet in the air. He continued to fly higher and higher. Suddenly, he was soaring like an eagle. As he rose into the heavens, he got a good look at the bird that had motivated him to fly higher.

Low and behold, the bird looked just like him. He was shocked to discover that he was an eagle and not a chicken. All his life he had been living below his ability because he had not discovered his true potential. He had been surrounded by chickens and had thought like a chicken.

His thought process held him back. It had kept him from rising above the crowd. He was living a life of mediocrity instead of fulfilling his superior destiny. Finally, he learned to think like an eagle and soar like an eagle because he was an eagle.

My friend, if you want to soar like an eagle, you cannot think like a chicken. Do not listen to the negative influences of this world. Do not look around you, learn to look above yourself. Look to God and let Him motivate your life. The Bible says in Isaiah 40:31:

But those who wait on the Lord shall renew their strength;
they shall mount up with wings like eagles, they shall run
and not be weary, they shall walk and not faint.

Yes, God has the spiritual power to energize your life. God can bless your life far beyond your wildest dreams. He will cause you to soar like and eagle to a level of living you once considered impossible. You will set your sights far above the level of mediocrity. God can enable you to reach for new horizons and fulfill your God-given potential.

First, you must be in proper relationship with God. The Scripture says in John 1:12:

But as many as received Him, to them He gave the right to become children of God, even to those who believe in His name.

Yes, you become a child of God by inviting Jesus into your life. Simply tell God that you believe Jesus died and rose again for your sins. Then place your faith and trust in Christ for the free gift of eternal life.

The Scripture says in Ephesians 2:8-9:

For by grace you have been saved through faith, and that not of yourselves; it is the gift of God, not of works, lest anyone should boast.

Once you have Christ in your life, you have all the benefits He offers. You will have forgiveness of sins, a home in heaven, and a new power for living in this world. God will help you discover your true potential. The Bible will come alive to you and prayer will take on a new meaning.

This will help you gain a positive focus and develop a positive attitude. Your life will take on a new meaning and a fresh sense of purpose. As you look to God, you will learn to soar like an eagle.

CHAPTER 6

HAPPINESS IS A
SPIRITUAL STATE OF MIND

Are you looking for happiness today? Well, there is good news for you. Jesus said in Matthew 5:6:

Blessed are those who hunger and thirst for righteousness, for they shall be filled.

You see, the word "blessed" means "happy, fortunate, satisfied or contented." Jesus says the way to be happy and satisfied is through hungering and thirsting for righteousness. Therefore, happiness is a spiritual state of mind.

You know, it has been said: "we are what we eat." We certainly understand that concept in physical terms. Let's face it, if we eat properly, we will have healthy bodies. However, if we eat poorly, our bodies will suffer. We may feel sluggish and experience fatigue. Our energy can drain away from poor eating habits. The body needs proper nutrition to function at peak performance.

Well, the same is true spiritually. In a very real sense, spiritually speaking, we are what we eat. The soul needs to digest good spiritual nutrition. We benefit greatly from a proper spiritual diet. We will experience positive spiritual energy from positive spiritual input.

The key is to develop a healthy spiritual appetite. Learn to read the Bible and pray that God will speak to your heart.

Claim the promise of Jesus when He said in Matthew 5:6:

Blessed are those who hunger and thirst for righteousness, for they shall be filled.

The word "filled" means "satisfied."

Just like a hungry man who is supplied with food is satisfied, so you will be spiritually satisfied as well. Just as a thirsty man in the desert is satisfied with a cool drink of water, so the word of God will satisfy your soul.

Read the four Gospels: Matthew, Mark, Luke, and John. Your soul will be satisfied as you catch a fresh glimpse of the Savior. Your heart will be comforted as you read of His love and compassion for people. Your soul will be blessed as you see Jesus demonstrate His omnipotent power.

You will be challenged to greater vision for your life as you read about the power of Christ. You will attempt to do the impossible as you hear Jesus say, "With God All Things Are Possible." You will refuse to accept the word impossible as you listen to Jesus say in His word, "For with God nothing will be impossible."

You will rise up with a fresh outlook on life as you hear Jesus say, "Have faith in God." Your soul will be renewed as you see the Master reach out His loving hand and give a healing touch to a hurting person. Your faith will be made strong as you read of Jesus calming the stormy sea by simply saying "Peace be still."

Oh my friend, hunger and thirst for a relationship with Jesus and you will be satisfied. Look to Jesus for your every need. He will never let you down.

The Bible tells us in Hebrews 12:2 to "look unto Jesus, the author and finisher of our faith, who for the joy that was set before Him endured the cross, despising the shame, and has sat down at the right hand of the throne of God."

Yes, Jesus can be depended upon for our every need. He died and rose again for our sins. It was a joy for Him to purchase our forgiveness with His sacrifice on the cross. While he suffered a painful death, he experienced the joy of reconnecting our broken relationship with God.

My friend, if you hunger and thirst for a right relationship with God, Jesus will satisfy your soul. Jesus said in John 6:35:

I am the bread of life. He who comes to Me shall never hunger, and he who believes in Me shall never thirst.

Jesus offers a rich and meaningful life. Your soul will be satisfied with a relationship with Christ. He offers meaning and purpose and direction in this life. Jesus will also show you a new way of living. Following Christ will mean that some things will need to change. However, it will be a change for the better.

Some people are afraid to study the Bible and follow the life of Christ. They fear that God will make them miserable as they submit to Biblical teaching. Therefore, when they come upon a command that is contrary to their lifestyle, they want to ignore it. They will not be able to see the good in making the right change of attitude or action.

However, if we hunger and thirst for a right relationship with God, we will want to live right as well. Therefore, we will better understand that God's commands are for our own good. Consequently, we will learn that the Bible is not a rulebook to make us miserable, it is a roadmap to make us successful.

The result will be positive. We will experience the joy of obedience and the satisfaction that Jesus offers to our soul. We will have a positive attitude toward scripture as we feast upon the Word of God. We will discover that "Happiness is a spiritual state of mind."

You know, I will never forget my first grade teacher. Her name was Mrs. Golden. She was an outstanding teacher and a wonderful lady. I have so many fond memories of her.

I'll never forget my first day of school. When I walked into the first grade classroom, Mrs. Golden smiled and said, "There's my little butterball lamby-pie." She was like a grandmother to me and I loved her. Mrs. Golden had taught for many years and was a very gifted teacher. She was "hooked on phonics" long before the hooked on phonics program was developed.

She was a strict disciplinarian and yet she had a gentle spirit. She taught us more than simply reading and writing. She taught us how to get along together.

Mrs. Golden was also a generous woman. Her husband had a cotton candy machine and once a year he would come to school and make cotton candy for the entire elementary school. It was always the highlight of the year.

I remember how Mrs. Golden would pray every day before lunch. We would bow our heads and she would thank the good Lord for our food and thank Him for our many blessings. I will never forget the day she stood before the class and told us she was no longer allowed to pray for our food. Tears rolled down her face as we sat in disbelief that people were actually outlawing prayer in school. It broke her heart. Therefore, it broke our little hearts as well.

Mrs. Golden was truly an incredible woman. She taught us the golden rule to "treat others as we would want to be treated." We learned so much more than the three R's from Mrs. Golden.

Mrs. Golden also had her own "golden rule" when it came to eating the school lunch. We had to taste two bites of any food we said we didn't want to eat. If you asked to leave an item on the lunch tray, she would always ask, "Have you taken two bites of the food?" If she doubted you, then she would make you eat two bites as observed you swallowing the food.

Believe me, we ate two bites of everything. Consequently, a strange thing happened that year as I learned to taste a variety of different foods. To my surprise, I discovered that I actually liked the taste of many foods I thought I would never eat. Looking back now, I can see that she had my best interest in mind.

My friend, in many ways, the commands of God are like that. We have a misconceived notion that it will be terrible to obey

Biblical teaching. However, God smiles and says, "Taste and see that the Lord is good."

Jesus says in Matthew 5:6:

Blessed are those who hunger and thirst for righteousness, for they shall be filled.

Once we submit to Christ as Savior and Lord, our perspective changes and our spiritual hunger increases. We develop an appetite for the Word of God and we become thirsty for the Spirit of God. We learn that only Jesus can satisfy the soul. Yes, when all is said and done, "Happiness is a spiritual state of mind."

CHAPTER 7

THE I AM
DETERMINES THE I CAN

I want to ask you a question. How do you view yourself? Your answer to that question could speak volumes concerning your potential for success. It is an accepted fact that a person's success or failure is often directly related to their self-image.

The Scripture says in Psalm 139:14:

I will praise You, for I am fearfully and wonderfully made; Marvelous are Your works, and that my soul knows very well.

Yes, God is our creator. He has created us for a purpose. Almighty God has a plan for your life. Viewing yourself as a special creation of God will give you the confidence you need to succeed in any area of your life. Paul said in Philippians 4:13:

I can do all things through Christ who strengthens me.

A healthy self-image and a positive self-esteem pave the way for a bright future. This person is not afraid to run the risk of failure in an attempt to succeed. A failure does not destroy them. It simply becomes a training ground and a stepping-stone to success.

However, someone with a poor self-image and low self-esteem is unwilling to take a chance to succeed. Fear of failure keeps them frozen in their tracks. They would rather continue on with the age old "status quo." After all, any attempt to achieve a goal means you also stand a chance to fail.

Therefore, it is easier to continue on the broad road of mediocrity instead of the narrow road of prosperity. However, the person who achieves greatness in any field of endeavor is often driven by a voice from within that says, "you were created by the Lord and you have that special something that will enable you to succeed." Yes, the I am determines the I can.

I am reminded of the story that is told concerning the 1977 New York Yankees, who were called "The Million Dollar Team." George Steinbrenner had grown weary of losing. He wanted to restore that great Yankee tradition of winning. The Yankees have a rich history of being a championship ball club and Steinbrenner was eager to bring back "Yankee pride" to the "Big Apple."

Consequently, Steinbrenner went out and purchased the best ball players that money could buy. Men like Reggie Jackson, Willie Randolph, Thurmond Munson, Chris Chambliss, and several other great ball players. The salaries skyrocketed as Steinbrenner put together his expensive team.

However, at the all-star break, the Yankees were nine games out of first place. Team spirit was low and dissension was high. Steinbrenner realized that it would take more than money to motivate this highly talented team.

Therefore, Steinbrenner called for a meeting of the team. They gathered in the locker room and waited for the explosive owner to speak. He walked in quietly and stood in silence as he stared at his million-dollar team. You could cut the tension with a knife.

Finally, Steinbrenner held up a Yankee uniform. He stood there holding the uniform and began speaking of the Yankee pinstripes. He told them how many teams had changed their style of uniforms but not the New York Yankees. You see, the pinstripes represented the rich history and the long standing winning tradition of the Yankees. He stood there like a rock holding the Yankee uniform with its pinstripes and spoke of many great ball players who wore the uniform in the past.

He began by describing Babe Ruth. After all, the Yankee Stadium is called "the house that Ruth built." Then he spoke of Lou Gerig, who was known as the "iron man." Steinbrenner went on to mention men like Joe DiMaggio, Yoggi Berra, Mickey

Mantle, and Roger Maris. After describing these incredible hall of famers, Steinbrenner looked his million dollar team in the eyes and shouted,"You wear the Yankee pinstripes! You are the New York Yankees! Play like New York Yankees!"

Then he turned and walked out of the locker room. The result, this million dollar team rallied the rest of the season and went on to win the World Series. Once they believed in who they were, they began to play like champions. Yes, the I am determines the I can.

My friend, this leads me back to my original question. How do you view yourself today? Do you see yourself as being created by God? Did you know that God loves you and has a wonderful plan for your life? That's right, God created you for the purpose of having fellowship with Him. You see, the Bible says you were created in the image of God. Genesis 1:27 says:

So God created man in His own image; in the image of God
He created him, male and female He created them.

To be created in the image of God means you have a mind to think, emotions to feel, and a will to choose. You are a rational being with a moral conscience. Consequently, you have the capacity to have fellowship with God.

To be created in the image of God is a tremendous honor. It adds an incredible value to your life and great meaning to your existence. Your self-image should be based on the fact that you have been designed by God. Your life was created for a divine purpose. Your self-esteem should be based on the concept that God is your creator. This means that your life has great value because you are important to God. Discovering this truth will produce great enthusiasm for your life.

You know, the New York Yankees were reminded of their great heritage as they wore their pinstripe uniforms. Their owner had a high expectation for them to represent the great Yankee winning tradition. In a similar way, our heavenly Father expects us to live up to our potential because we are created in the image of God. Make no mistake about it my friend, the I am determines the I can.

CHAPTER 8

CHOOSE TO BE AN INSPIRATION—
NOT AN IRRITATION

Let me ask you a question: What kind of a person have you decided to be in the future? Think about it. How we live our life really boils down to the decisions we choose to make. It has been said that, "Life is not made of the dreams we dream, but in the decisions we make." Therefore, let me encourage you to make a positive decision today. Choose to be an inspiration not an irritation.

You might be asking, how can I choose to be an inspiration to others? Well, I think we all know the kinds of things that irritate people. We often deal with that and it certainly needs little, if any, explanation at all.

However, what about being an inspiration? What types of things inspire others? I believe we can inspire people using three basic principles - Faith, hope and love.

The Bible says in I Corinthians 13:13:

And now abide faith, hope, love, these three, but the greatest of these is love.

First of all, people who seek to inspire others will build up their positive faith. It has been said that faith inspires success. I like the way Paul Harvey puts it. He says, "I've never seen a monument erected to a pessimist." That's right, much of life boils down to our perspective on life. You can either see the glass as half full or half empty. It simply comes down to how we choose to view things.

Make no mistake about it, if we choose to be a pessimist, we will irritate our own human spirit and the hearts of those around us. However, if we choose to be an optimist, we will encourage others and ourselves as well. Build faith in others and you will be an inspiration to people. People will like you and want to spend time with you.

Positive faith is an inspiration and faith inspires success. Jesus said in Matthew 17:20:

I say to you, if you have faith as a mustard seed, you will say to this mountain, 'Move from here to there,' and it will move; and nothing will be impossible for you.

My friend, positive faith is mountain-moving faith. You will come into contact with people who will face challenges that seem like mountains.Choose to be an inspiration to these people. Help them see that through faith in God, mountains can be scaled over, tunneled through, gone around, or possibly even cast into the sea. Obstaacles can be totally removed. Help them follow the advice of Jesus as found in Mark 11:22 where He says, "Have faith in God."

The first principle in being an inspiration to others is to build them up with a positive faith. Secondly, we need to encourage others with hope. Never underestimate the power of hope. After all, hope sustains success. When people are motivated by the power of hope they gain momentum to succeed.

You see this principle in football all the time. One team is trailing another team. It looks as if the game is almost over. Then comes a big play. A blocked punt, an interception for a touchdown, a recovered fumble, or a kick-off return for a touchdown. Whatever the case may be, all of a sudden the momentum shifts from that big play.

The events that follow can almost be predicted. One team begins to smell the hope of a comeback. They can feel the excitement in the air. The other team begins to fear they will lose their lead. Their hope begins to dwindle.

The end result? Hope becomes the inspiration for the comeback. They believe they can win and they do. Faith inspires the success, while hope sustains the success. People do not throw in the towel as long as there is hope.

That is one reason why Christians can persevere in life's trials. We have the sustaining power of the blessed hope of our Lord's return. The Scripture says in Titus 2:13:

looking for the blessed hope and the glorious appearing of our great God and Savior Jesus Christ.

Yes, hope gives the power of perseverance. Hope sustains success. You can be an inspiration to others as you encourage others with hope.

Lastly, you will be an inspiration to others as you lift them up with love. People who demonstrate love for others will build the foundation for a trusting relationship. Love says, "I will make your problem, my problem." Love sanctifies success because love deals with our motive of service. The Bible says, "love never fails."

My friend, we can never show too much love in this world. People need to know that God loves them and you love them too. The Bible says in I John 4:8 that God is love! The Bible tells us in John 3:16:

For God so loved the world that He gave His only begotten Son, that whoever believes in Him should not perish but have everlasting life.

Yes, God loves you today.

He wants you to be an inspiration to others by sharing His love. The love of God was a sacrificial love as He gave His Son for us. Yes, we can be an inspiration to others, as we become a channel for God's love to flow through us.

Bottom line, you can either be a balcony dweller or a basement dweller. A balcony dweller will lift people up to a higher level of living. These people focus on the positive aspects of life and inspire people with encouragement. They lift the spirit of others up and energize people for success.

Basement dwellers, on the other hand, always drag people down. They focus on the negative and continually find fault with everything. This causes a spirit of depression and drains people of energy. Believe me, you will be able to tell the difference between a balcony dweller and a basement dweller.

Yes, you can choose to be an inspiration and not an irritation to others. People who are committed to the Word of God will build others up in the faith. People who are confident in the power of God will encourage others with hope. People who are a channel of God's compassion will lift others up with love.

Yes, through faith, hope, and love, you can choose to be an inspiration, not an irritation.

CHAPTER 9

FAITH SAYS, "GO FOR IT"

Let me ask you a question. Are you the kind of person who can say "Go for it" or do you say "Hang on to it"? It really boils down to an outlook on life. If you are confident and secure in Christ, you can have the courage to say, "Go for it." Take the calculated risk. Be willing to put it all on the line for a shot at even greater success. After all, faith says, "Go for it."

On the other hand, fear says, "Hang on to it." Don't take the chance of losing what you have for a greater opportunity. Decisions based on fear have insecurity and the fear of failure at the heart of the matter.

Don't misunderstand me. I'm not talking about throwing caution to the wind. However, I am talking about living your life to the fullest; having enough confidence in yourself to fulfill your God-given potential. George S. Patton said, "Take calculated risks. That is different from being rash."

Basically, faith looks at the opportunity for success. However, fear looks at the potential failure. Faith looks at the satisfaction of conquering the mountain. While fear looks at the way the mountain can conquer you. Faith says, "Go for it." Faith reaches for your dreams. Fear, on the other hand, is afraid to dream because it could turn into a nightmare.

My friend, in a nutshell, faith motivates you from a positive mindset while fear is a negative force. Faith seeks to catch the vision of increase, while fear seeks to only reduce your losses.

The Bible says in Hebrews 11:1:

Now faith is the substance of things hoped for, the evidence of things not seen.

You see, faith in God does not mean everything will be spelled out for you. God is saying that faith involves taking an apparent calculated risk. It is only an apparent risk because God can always be trusted. Consequently, there is nothing to fear. That's why the Bible says in II Timothy 1:7:

For God has not given us a spirit of fear, but of power and of love and of a sound mind.

God does not want us to live a life based on fear. After all, fear will produce negative emotions, which will drain your strength. Fear will cripple your power of creativity. However, faith will release a positive energy, which will give you triumph over life's trials. Faith will give you the courage to say, "I'm going for it" because: "I can do all things through Christ who strengthens me."

My friend, don't stand still and watch life go by. Get involved in this thing called "living by faith" and make a difference in your world. The late John F. Kennedy once said, "One person can make a difference and every person should try."

Faith in God will enable you to make a difference in your world. Faith will motivate you with a positive passion to fulfill your God-given purpose. Jesus said in John 15:8, "by this My Father is glorified, that you bear much fruit."

Yes, God has designed for you to bear fruit for His glory. Fruit for God is everything from demonstrating positive character traits, to encouraging the downhearted, to pointing someone to the Savior. The key to bearing fruit for Christ is found in abiding in Christ.

Jesus said in John 15:7:

If you abide in Me, and My words abide in you, you will ask what you desire, and it shall be done for you.

To abide in Christ is to spend time with Him through prayer, Bible study, and worship. This will build your faith. It will enable you to move from a "hanging on" mentality to a "go for it" mover and shaker for God's glory.

Faith will enable you to risk failure because your security is in Jesus Christ. Faith will cause you to cry out, "If God is for me, who can be against me."

Here's the bottom line. Ten years from now do you want to look back and say, "I wish I had," or "I'm glad I did?" People filled with faith have the confidence to be courageous in life.

Consequently, faith thinkers often become "over-achievers." Faith thinkers become "extra-ordinary people" in an ordinary world. Faith thinkers become "go for it" people and achieve greatness.

The world is a better place because of faith thinkers. Anyone can say, "Hang on to it." However, "go for it" people instill faith in others with a positive enthusiasm, which is contagious.

"Go for it" people are "I'm glad I did it" people. They don't look and say, "I wish I had." Their faith in God brought success because they courageously "went for it."

Let me tell you about a lady who went for it. Her husband had died and left her with very little. She was a heartbroken widow faced with the challenge to go on. She had a decision to make, would she wallow in self-doubt and self-pity or would she pick up the pieces of her shattered life.

You can imagine the pain she felt and the tears that fell from her broken heart. The love of her life was gone. Never again would she wake up in the morning to his smiling face. Never again would they relax together in the evening. They would never again be able to enjoy simple things like "sipping a hot cup of coffee by the warm fireplace." Never again would they enjoy a glass of iced tea as they sat on the back patio and watched the sun drift out of sight.

Yes, her heart was broken, but what would she do. Her only asset was the one little candy store that her husband had owned and operated. Now the candy store was in her lap.

Should she decide to "hang on to what she had" or "go for it" with faith and the courage to succeed? Would she be driven by fear or motivated by faith?

Well, this dear lady decided to not sit around and feel sorry for herself and grow old in bitterness. She went down to the candy store with a fierce determination. Her faith caused her to "go for it." She decided to improve upon the candy store and invent some new chocolates. She made several new recipes, which were well received by her customers. The candy store began to take off like "wild fire."

Consequently, she opened another and another and so on. She kept inventing new recipes and opening more candy stores.

The end result was a nationwide candy store chain. Yes, "Fannie May" decided to have a faith which said "go for it." She was not content to simply hold on to what she had. Oh no, not Fannie May. She was able to look back and say, "I'm glad I did."

My friend, pursue your dream and always remember: Faith says, "Go for it."

Chapter 10

Hope Says, "I'll Make It"

Psalm 71:5 says:

For You are my hope, O Lord God; You are my trust from my youth.

Yes, hope says, "I'll make it." After all, our hope is in the Lord. The Scripture tells us in Romans 4:4 that perseverance produces character and character produces hope.

Yes, hope gives us the courage to remain committed. Hope produces positive motivation and builds momentum toward success. Hope says, "I'll stick it out because eventually things will swing in my direction." Faith believes the mountain will be removed and hope hangs on until it happens. Faith inspires success and hope sustains success.

My friend, the real movers and shakers of this world have a fire burning in their soul. They have a passion to help people stretch and grow into greatness. High achievers know the fine line between average and excellence. Hope motivates this person to stretch for success. Faith will cause you to pursue your dreams and hope will sustain your efforts.

For example, Roger Staubach was certainly one of the greatest quarterbacks to ever play the game of football. He was not only an outstanding player, but he was a great leader, as well. He had a passion to be the very best he could be.

Roger also had to overcome come incredible odds. You see, he played college football at the Naval Academy. This meant he would have to serve four years in the Navy following graduation. He was an outstanding college quarterback. In fact, in his junior year, he won the Heisman Trophy. He had a tremendous throwing ability and completed 67% of his passes. It was a phenomenal year.

However, no one thought he could make it in the pros. No one had ever made a successful return to football following four years of military service. Therefore, Roger Staubach knew it would take total dedication to achieve his goal.

During the next four years, Roger Staubach served in the Navy. At the same time, he worked with a fierce determination. He ran, lifted weights and trained hard. He forced himself through a brutal work out each and every day.

He also kept his arm sharp and passing eye keen. He threw 400 passes each and every day for four years. He threw passes on the deck of an aircraft carrier and on the dusty roads of Vietnam.

In 1969, Roger Staubach was a 27-year-old rookie for Tom Landry and the Dallas Cowboys. He was the third string quarterback. Two outstanding veteran quarterbacks were in front of him. The odds were very slim for Roger Staubach to play much in the pros.

However, Roger Staubach loved the game and his desire to play was driven by the power of hope. His passion continued to drive him for the goal of excellence. After practice, Staubach would stay on the field and throw to the young receivers. When they would literally drop from exhaustion, Staubach would sprint to the locker room.

His love for the game pushed him beyond human limitations. He would lift weights with unrelenting desire. When the players would collapse, Staubach would do five more reps. His passion was an inspiration to all.

Finally, he got a shot at the number one quarterback position. Landry could not hold back the heavily driven Staubach. My friend, the rest is history. He went on to become one of the greatest quarterbacks in the history of pro football. The reason was simple. His hope sustained his success and gave him the confidence to say, "I'll make it."

By the way, Roger Staubach is also a Christian. He has a personal relationship with God through faith in Jesus Christ. I am confident that he would agree with Romans 5:5 that says, "Now hope does not disappoint, because the love of God has been poured out in our hearts by the Holy Spirit who was given to us."

My friend, look to Jesus and place your faith in Him. Keep your hope in the Lord and you will conquer any challenge. After all, Hope says, "I'll make it."

CHAPTER 11

LOVE SAYS, "I WILL GIVE IT MY ALL"

The Scripture tells us in I Corinthians 13:8 that, "love never fails." Love in action is "making your problem, my problem." Love purifies our motive and sanctifies our success.

Jesus said in John 15:13:

Greater love has no one than this, than to lay down one's life for his friends.

Yes, sacrificial love will motivate us to put everything on the line for a great cause.

The Scripture tells us in I John 4:11:

Beloved, if God so loved us, we also ought to love one another.

Our love for others should be motivated by the realization that God loves us. Following the example of the sacrificial love of God will empower you to apply great sacrifice to achieve great success. In essence, love says, "I will give it my all."

I'm reminded of the incredible story of sacrificial love that took place several years ago. It was September 24, 1986, in Crystal River, Florida. Twelve-year-old, Michael Morgret, and his four-teen-year-old cousin, Kelly Thomas, were snorkeling in a pond behind the Morgret home. It was a hot evening and the two cousins were enjoying their refreshing swim.

Across the pond, Dr. Fernandez was relaxing in his easy chair. He looked out his picture window and watched the two boys, who were swimming together. Perhaps his mind thought back to when he was a kid and life was "carefree." He probably reflected on the days when he and his friends used to cool off in the local "swimming hole."

Suddenly, he was brought to the shocking reality that life is not always "foot loose and fancy free." Dr. Fernandez was horrified as he spotted an enormous alligator enter the pond. He could not believe his eyes. The deadly alligator was quietly making its way toward the two unsuspecting boys.

Dr. Fernandez leaped to his feet and ran wildly out of the house toward the pond. He screamed at the boys, but their heads were under water as they snorkeled in the pond. He began shouting and clapping wildly at the edge of the pond. He wanted to alert the boys and also divert the attention of the alligator. However, his efforts were futile.

Then, Kelly Thomas surfaced and heard the commotion. He shouted at his cousin to swim to shore. Kelly swam safely to the shore, but Michael Morgret's afternoon was about to become a life and death situation.

Michael still had his head under water and was completely unaware of his dangerous situation. His mother, Jesse Morgret, was doing dishes at the kitchen sink when she heard the commotion. She looked out the window and her heart froze with terror. She saw an enormous alligator heading straight for her son. The alligator latched onto the head and shoulders of Michael Morgret. The alligator surfaced on its tail and Jesse Morgret saw her son's waist and legs dangling from the mouth of the gator.

The alligator then took the boy to the bottom of the pond. Often times, they will store their prey under the water and return to eat it a couple of days later. At the bottom of the pond, the alligator spit out Michael Morgret. He surfaced to the top of the water and was completely dazed. He literally had no idea what had hit him.

His mother, cousin, and the neighbor across the pond screamed at him to swim to shore. The twelve-year-old boy spotted the alligator and realized his danger. He began a swim for his life to the shore, where his mother was standing.

He was almost to shore when the alligator latched on to his legs from behind. Again, the gator surfaced on its tail and was about to head for deep water. The boy was so close to safety and now it looked like he would surely die.

However, what took place in the next few minutes is the amazing story of the power of love. It would almost be unbelievable if Dr. Fernandez had not witnessed the action with his own eyes. The mother of the boy leaped into the pond and grabbed on to the outstretched hands of her son.

For the next few minutes a wrestling match took place between a five-foot, ninety-eight pound mother and an eleven-foot, four hundred pound alligator. Jesse Morgret dug her fingers to the bone in the back of her son's hands. She held on with the supernatural power of a mother motivated by love. She clung to her son and absolutely refused to let go. She was either going to save her son or die trying.

All of a sudden, the alligator let go and Jesse Morgret pulled her son from the jaws of death. The alligator swam away and was later killed by the authorities. It measured eleven feet in length and weighed four hundred pounds.

Jesse Morgret had proved that love says, "I'll give it my all." In fact, she left two scars on the back of her son's hands that are referred to as "love scars." They are the loving reminder of a mother who dug her fingers to the bone to rescue her child.

My friend, that reminds me of the love of Jesus. After all, our life was helplessly trapped in the jaws of sin. We were completely without hope and in need of a Savior. Therefore, Jesus gave His life as a sacrifice on the cross to rescue us from our sins. He left heaven and came to this earth for the purpose of the cross. Romans 5:8 says,

But God demonstrates His own love toward us, in that while we were still sinners, Christ died for us.

Yes, it was love that drove Him to the cross and love never fails. Nails did not keep Him on the cross, love did. Jesus demonstrated the ultimate sacrifice of love when He died on the cross for our sins. Today, Jesus has the "love scars" in His hands and feet as visible proof of His love for all of humanity.

The Scripture tells us in I Corinthians 13:13:

And now abide faith, hope, love, these three; but the greatest of these is love.

Yes, Faith says, "Go For It."

Hope says, "I'll Make it".

Love says, "I'll Give It My All."

I trust that you will "Go For It" with your faith in Jesus. May hope remind you that, "You'll Make It." May love motivate you to "Give It Your All" in worship of Christ.

CHAPTER 12

THE CROSS IS THE MESSAGE OF LOVE

Romans 5:8 says:

But God demonstrates His own love toward us, in that while we were still sinners, Christ died for us.

Yes, make no mistake about it; the cross is a message of love.

The Roman Crucifixion was the cruelest form of execution ever devised by man. It was reserved for the vilest offenders. It was designed to be a slow and agonizing death. The purpose was to inflict as much pain as possible as the victim was openly and publicly tortured to death. It was so brutal that men literally begged for mercy.

It began with a whipping by what is known as the "cat-o'-nine-tails." This was a leather ball attached to the end of a whip. Sticking out of the leather ball were spikes of steel and glass. This would literally tear the flesh right off a man's back.

The one who gave the whipping was schooled in the art of this violent punishment. He was highly trained to inflict pain completely without mercy. Thirty-nine stripes were the maximum by Roman law and every lash was included.

The man giving the whipping would bring the cat of nine tails down on a persons back and then snap his wrist and pull the whip down. This was a ruthless act and would tear a man's back to shreds. All of the layers of skin would be torn off a man's back as he cried out for mercy, but no mercy was given. They would be tied to a pole because their legs would collapse from the incredible pain. By the 39th stripe you could literally pull back the flesh and see the backbones of the victim of this torturous execution.

Following the brutal whipping would come the actual crucifixion itself. The person would be slammed onto the cross where splinters would now enter the flesh on his back. Nails would be driven into his hands and feet to secure him to the cross. The person would be hung naked on the cross in order to increase the total humiliation. You can imagine the pain and the agony an individual would endure. It was truly a horrible and gruesome death. However, the agony had only begun.

Once the cross was raised, a new sense of pain and suffering would kick in. As the person hung on the cross the body would slump down. This caused the air supply to be cut off from the lungs. Consequently, the person would begin to suffocate. Therefore, the natural reaction of the body would instinctively push up with his feet to raise the body for air. This would in turn send excruciating pain through the feet. Back and forth between suffocation and horrible pain from the spikes in the hands and feet. The individual would go through this process for hours and sometimes even for a couple of days before he would die. The crucifixion was a horrible, cruel, brutal, and agonizing way to die.

My friend, that is the death that Jesus Christ died. The question must be asked, why would Jesus go through that kind of agony? The answer is this: The cross is a message of love. Jesus gave His life as a sacrifice for our sins and the ultimate demonstration of unconditional love.

You see my friend; sin had severed our relationship with God. However, God chose to restore our relationship through the sacrifice of His own Son on the cross for our sins. Jesus laid down His life in order to offer us the free gift of eternal life.

The Bible says in John 3:16:

For God so loved the world that He gave His only begotten Son, that whoever believes in Him should not perish but have everlasting life.

Yes, God loves you today. The cross clearly reveals the amazing love of God. Jesus stretched out His arms on the cross as a symbol of His open arms to humanity.

Jesus said in John 15:13:

Greater love has no one than this, than to lay down one's life for his friends.

That's right, we have the opportunity to experience not only forgiveness from Christ, but also His friendship. The Bible says that Jesus is a friend that sticks closer than a brother. His friendship is not based on the law of God. It is founded on the love of God.

Yes, the symbol of the Christian faith is not two tablets of stone. No, the law of God is not the answer to our needs. The symbol of the Christian faith is the cross. The reason is simple; the love of God is what we need. The good news is the cross reminds us that the love of God is available to us.

I John 4:10 says:

In this is love, not that we loved God, but that He loved us and sent His Son to be the satisfaction for our sins.

Yes, God is love and the cross is a message of His love. That is why the Bible states, "behold what manner of love the Father has bestowed on us." The cross is an incredible demonstration of the depth of the love of God for us. The Bible goes on to say, "By this we know love, because He laid down His life for us." The Scripture also says, "We love Him because He first loved us."

My friend, have you experienced the love of God today? Do you feel His presence and His comfort? Have you tasted and seen that the Lord is good? Have you listened to the message of love that cries out from the cross? Jesus loves you today. His love was proven yesterday, is a reality today, and His love is secure for your tomorrow. The cross is a tremendous message of the incredible love of God.

In London there is a chapel known as the Charing Cross. You see, years ago the beloved wife of the King died far away from London. As the king tenderly and lovingly brought her body back to the city of London, he built chapels along the way. Wherever they would stop and rest on the long journey, the king would erect a small chapel.

Each of these chapels would bear a special name. The Kings Cross or the Charing Cross, etc. Over the years, the Charing Cross Chapel in London began to be referred to simply as "The Cross."

Several years later, a little girl became lost in the streets of London. She wandered around helplessly trying to find her home. An English police officer found her sobbing and offered to help her find her way home.

However, the little girl did not remember her address. The tears streamed down her face as her little heart began to break. The police officer comforted her and explained that all would be well.

He sat down on the curb beside the little girl and offered a simple plan. He said, "I'll name some places in London and you tell me if you recognize any of them." He mentioned "Piccadilly Circus?" The little girl responded, "No." He asked if she was aware of "Westminster." Again she responded, "No." Finally, he asked if she knew of "Charing Cross." "Ah", said the little girl with tears in her eyes. "Yes, yes, take me to the cross and I can find my way home from there."

My friend, how true it is for all of humanity. Simply go to the cross and you can find your way home to God from there. Jesus died on the cross for our sins and rose again the third day for our sins.

He is the answer for your every need. He gives hope for the broken heart. He provides healing for the wounded soul. Jesus gives forgiveness to the person who trusts in Him. Open up your heart to the love of God through faith in Jesus Christ. Yes, the cross is a message of love.

CHAPTER 13

JESUS IS A RISEN SAVIOR AND VICTORIOUS LORD

My friend, the resurrection of Christ is a victorious message. It is the resurrection that separates Christianity from all other religions. If you check the tomb of Buddha, you will still find him there. If you check the tomb of Mohammed, you will still find him there. However, if you check the tomb of Jesus, you will not find Him there. Jesus is a risen Savior and victorious Lord.

The angel made the announcement at the empty tomb. Mark 16:6 says:

But he said to them, 'Do not be alarmed. You seek Jesus of Nazareth, who was crucified. He is risen! He is not here. See the place where they laid Him.'

Yes my friend, the most powerful words in all of history are: He is risen!

Humanity was groping in darkness. Death had reigned throughout human history. Romans 5:12 says:

Therefore, just as through one man sin entered the world, and death through sin, and thus death spread to all men, because all sinned.

Yes, people throughout history have death as a common denominator. However, we find that Jesus was another story. He left heaven and came to this earth as the perfect Son of God. He never sinned. He was perfect in every way. He was the sinless Son of God, the unique God-man.

His destiny was the cross. He suffered on the cross for our sins. He experienced the guilt of the world on the cross. He literally went through hell on the cross as He suffered alone. God the Father turned His back on the Son of God. Darkness covered the land as Jesus was separated from His Father. In agony, our Lord cried out, *My God, My God, Why have you forsaken Me?*

Evil men mocked Him and cursed Him. They beat Him and spat upon Him. He wore a crown of thorns crushed into His bleeding brow. He went through a mockery of a trial and was falsely charged. They gave the awful sentence of crucifixion. Jesus was nailed to the old rugged cross and shed His blood for our sins. All of His disciples had forsaken Him in fear. The pain and agony and the complete aloneness was staggering.

Finally Jesus died on the cross. John 19:30 says:

So when Jesus had received the sour wine, He said, 'It is finished!' And bowing His head, He gave up His spirit.

Yes, it looked like death had claimed another victory. Jesus was removed from the cross and placed in a borrowed tomb. It was a sad, sad hour indeed.

The disciples were heartbroken. Their Lord had been taken from them. All of their hopes had been crushed. Their dreams of a better world and a bright tomorrow were shattered. Confusion and sorrow was the atmosphere of this earth shaking experience.

Where would they go? What would they do? Was there any hope for the future? It seemed like the cold and cruel grave would once again be the victor. Who would escape the clutches of the jaws of death? The vice grip of death's agony had put the squeeze on another victim.

However, tragedy would be turned into TRIUMPH. The scars from the cross would soon be turned into stars for a crown. The wounds in the Savior would be healing for the seeker. The separation from the Father would provide reconciliation for all of the Lord's followers.

You see my friend, three days after the crucifixion was the resurrection of our Lord. Yes, Jesus stepped out of the tomb. He had conquered the grave. The greatest victory in all of history took place when Jesus arose from the dead. I Corinthians 15:57 says:

> *But thanks be to God, who gives us the victory through our Lord Jesus Christ.*

Praise God today that Jesus is a risen Savior and victorious Lord. Colossians 2:15 says:

> *Having disarmed principalities and powers, He made a public spectacle of them, triumphing over them in it.*

Yes, Jesus delivered the crushing blow to the head of Satan at the cross. As the nails were driven into the hands and feet of Jesus, He was delivering the deathblow to the devil!

My friend, because of the victory of Jesus there is hope for any situation. You may be experiencing the heartache of a broken relationship. You may be wondering, is there hope? You may be under the strain of financial pressure. Perhaps you have climbed the ladder of success and discovered it is leaning against the wrong wall. You may be experiencing rejection and sorrow from a loved one who has walked away from you.

Maybe you have experienced a strained relationship with a close friend. Perhaps you have gone through the guilt of sin and need forgiveness. You may be asking, is their hope? Does God have an answer for you?

My friend, the Resurrection of Christ cries out today: YES, THERE IS HOPE. Jesus is alive and well. Jesus has conquered sin, death and hell itself by resurrecting from the dead. Jesus is a risen Savior and victorious Lord.

You know, several years ago a ship sank off the shores of New England. The boat capsized and left the crew in a disoriented state. The men began a frantic attempt to stay alive. They scrambled through the overturned ship in hope of escape.

Panic began to grip the hearts of these men who desperately wanted to stay alive. Many thought of their wife and children and wanted to live. The boat was rapidly filling with water. Time was running short and the situation was desperate.

It was the type of emergency that was the nightmare of every sailor. The ocean that had been their lifelong friend was quickly becoming their fatal enemy. The sea was claiming the lives of many men. Death was truly no respector of persons.

You can imagine the struggle for life during the panic stricken hour. Hearts were gripped with fear as the men struggled for survival. They were literally fighting for their lives.

It seemed like the death angel had placed one hand on their foot as they fought to climb for safety. Death was like an unwanted anchor pulling them down as they fought with all their might to live.

Finally, a few of the men found their way to the top of the capsized boat. They discovered an air pocket and hung on for their lives. They simply waited and wondered if help would come. You can only imagine their feeling of utter hopelessness.

Meanwhile, the coast guard began a desperate rescue attempt. They launched an all out search for the capsized boat. They fought through the raging storm searching for any sign of life.

Finally, on the third day of the rescue attempt, the divers located the sunken ship. They came upon the sunken ship and expected all to be lost. They figured that no one could have survived such an experience. However, the divers checked out the boat anyway. Suddenly the divers heard tapping from the sunken ship. They listened carefully and discovered the tapping was Morse Code. The men in the capsized boat were tapping: IS THERE HOPE?

The divers tapped back: YES, THERE IS HOPE! Knowing there was hope, the men hung on and were rescued. They experienced a glorious reunion with their loved ones.

My friend, all of humanity cries out today: IS THERE HOPE? Can anyone make a difference in our life? Can the problems of this world be solved? Can the emptiness of the human heart be filled?

Well my friend, the Resurrection of Jesus Christ answers back: YES, THERE IS HOPE! The resurrection of Jesus is a thunderous answer for all problems of all time. No situation is hopeless because of Jesus.

He died and rose again for our sins. He gives the free gift of eternal life to anyone who believes in Him. Simply place your total trust in Christ and Christ alone. Remember my friend; Jesus is a risen Savior and victorious Lord.

CHAPTER 14

JESUS IS IN THE LIFE CHANGING BUSINESS

Jesus is in the life changing business. Jesus said in John 3:3 "Unless one is born again, he cannot see the kingdom of God." In other words, if someone wants to go to heaven, they need a personal encounter with Jesus Christ. I think everyone wants to go to heaven. The question is, How do we get there?

I'm reminded of the story Billy Graham tells of an experience he had early in his ministry. He arrived in a small town where he was scheduled to preach that evening. He wanted to mail a letter so Billy Graham asked a young boy where the post office was located.

The boy told Billy Graham where the post office was located and Billy thanked the young boy. Billy then said to the boy: "If you'll come to the Baptist Church this evening, you can hear me tell everyone how to get to heaven." The boy responded, "No thanks, I don't think I'll come and hear you tell people how to get to heaven; after all, you don't even know your way to the post office."

Well, there is certainly some humor in that little story. However, we do need to know how to get to heaven. Jesus said in John 3:3 that we need to be "born again" in order to go to heaven.

The phrase "born again" is used by all kinds of people in various ways. The athlete who gets a second chance may say, "I feel born again." Johnny Mathes had a song out a few years ago - one of the lines said, "When I'm in your arms, I feel born again". In the 1980's movie "Tough Guys," starring Burt Lancaster and Kirk Douglas, they were being released from prison. Lancaster, who played Harry Doyle, turned to Kirk Douglas, who played Archie Long, and said, "I feel born again, Archie." Yes, after serving 30 years in prison he now felt "born again."

The idea is a fresh start. A new lease on life. Starting over with a clean slate. The past is behind and the future looks bright. It is the concept of "turning over a new leaf."

However, the question before us today is not what the term "born again" means to others, but what did Jesus intend for it to mean? To understand this we need to look at the context of the setting when Christ taught this important phrase "born again." We find it in the third chapter of John's gospel.

The Scripture says in John 3:1-3:

There was a man of the Pharisees named Nicodemus, a ruler of the Jews. This man came to Jesus by night and said to Him, 'Rabbi, we know that You are a teacher come from God; for no one can do these signs that You do unless God is with him.' Jesus answered and said to him, 'Most assuredly, I say to you, unless one is born again, he cannot see the kingdom of God.'

A few things need to be noted from this passage. First, Jesus was talking to a very religious man. The Bible says that Nicodemus was a Pharisee and a ruler of the Jews. The Pharisees were among the religious leaders of the day. They followed the commandments to the very letter of the law. They had their list of "do's and don'ts" and followed them very closely.

Nicodemus was even a ruler of the Jews. This means that he would have been one of the leading Pharisees. He was a highly religious man and people really looked up to him.

Outwardly, Nicodemus had it all together. He gave no indication to religious people that he needed anything. He was a highly moral man and certainly esteemed with high regard in the religious community.

Nicodemus also spoke well of Jesus Christ. He calls Him a teacher who was sent from God. He also pats Christ on the back "so to speak" concerning the Lord's miracles. In other words, Nicodemus was saying, "Jesus, I think you are a great man and a great teacher." Humanly speaking, everything sounds good. After all, here is a religious man who thinks highly of Jesus Christ. Certainly this man would be thought well of by Jesus Christ.

Yet Jesus Christ makes His amazing statement of our need to be born again to this highly religious man. What the Lord is saying to Nicodemus is clear and simple. He is saying, "Nicodemus, I'm not interested in your track record. Eternal life is the result of receiving the gift of God, not of our doing good things for God."

Jesus Christ was cutting it straight with this guy. He was forcing Nicodemus to deal with the need of a spiritual rebirth. Even though someone may do good things and even be very religious and think Christ is a good teacher, this is still not enough.

Yes, eternal life comes when we stop trying to earn it and simply receive it as God's gift. In fact, as you follow this passage of scripture, you will find the gift of eternal life is taught very clearly.

In fact, John 3:16, the greatest verse in the entire Bible, is in response to this man Nicodemus. "For God so loved the world that he gave His only begotten Son, that whoever believes in Him should not perish, but have everlasting life." Jesus is saying to Nicodemus, "I love you. I will die and raise again for you. Simply believe in me and you will have eternal life. Stop working for it and simply receive it as a gift."

The greatest news is found in the word "world". Yes, God loves each and every one of us. We are valuable to God. We are important enough for God to give His only Son to die on the cross for our sins. He made it possible for anyone to be born again. My friend, that is love beyond explanation. It is the matchless love of God.

You know, I believe Nicodemus became a believer in Christ, because in John 19:39, he is there helping bury the body of Jesus. This indicates that he became a follower of Christ. Can't you imagine how he rejoiced three days later when Christ stepped out of the grave?

I can almost hear the Lord saying, "Nicodemus, here I am, risen from the dead just like I told you I would." Nicodemus, your "born again" experience is real! My friend, it will be real for you today as well.

When we receive Christ into our life by faith, we become a new person spiritually. God wipes the slate clean. He gives us New Life. God places His Holy Spirit into our life for assurance and direction. We begin reading the Bible and can understand it. In fact, we hunger for the teachings of the Scriptures. Our church attendance and the Worship of God take on a whole new meaning. There is joy in our hearts and praise on our lips.

The New Birth is real. It is the clear teaching of Jesus Christ. It began with Nicodemus and it is still reaching people today. I know because Jesus has transformed my life. In fact, people who knew me as a teenager are usually surprised to find out that I am now a pastor.

You see, I was a rebellious young man who wanted nothing to do with God. I wanted to live my life my own way. I felt like I had seen so much hypocrisy in the church that I did not want anything to do with Christianity.

In fact, at the age of sixteen I boldly told a youth worker to never talk to me about the Christian faith again. I was outraged as I drove away from my meeting with him. I could not believe that he wasted an evening of my time to talk to me about Christianity. After our discussion, I figured I would never hear from him again.

However, he did something that I could not stop. He and a friend prayed for me every day for the next two years. After all, it has been said that, "talking to people for God is a great thing, but talking to God for people is even greater."

Well, to make a long story short, at the age of eighteen, I came under the conviction of my need of Christ. Late one night, I drove to my oldest brother's house and told him that I needed to be saved. Therefore, we knelt in prayer and I invited Christ into my life as my personal Lord and Savior. I am grateful to God that Jesus changed my life. In fact, even the two youth workers who had prayed for me were shocked at the transformation.

My friend, if you are not certain that you have been "born again", let me invite you to make sure today. Simply bow your head and tell God that you believe Christ died and rose again for your sins. Through a simple prayer of faith, you can invite Christ to come into your life and you will be born again. I can tell you from personal experience that you will never regret it. After all, Jesus is in the life changing business and He always changes our life for the better.

CHAPTER 15

TEAMWORK MEANS:
INDIVIDUAL SACRIFICE FOR TEAM SUCCESS

I believe a true champion in life is a person of character. It has been said: "Talent may get you to the top but it takes character to keep you there." Yes, people who achieve lasting success in life develop the foundation of character.

We need people of principle in leadership. We need people who will not sacrifice their values to gain a victory. A "win at all cost" mentality will often create a loser in the game of life.

I believe that teamwork is an important quality of the character of a champion. I define teamwork as "Individual sacrifice for team success." Jesus said in Mark 3:25 "A house divided against itself cannot stand."

Yes, people must work together to have a successful team. In essence, life is all about teamwork. A family is a team. Parents and children must learn to respect each other and get along together. Love in the home is often demonstrated by individual sacrifice for team success.

Many times parents give up their own desires to meet the needs of the children. It's called "responsibility." Parents work hard and deny themselves in order to provide for the ones they love. Children of character will learn to appreciate the sacrifice of mom and dad. Parents of character will not walk away from those depending on them. However, if everyone pursues their own way, the home will fall apart. After all Jesus said: "A house divided against itself cannot stand."

A home that defines teamwork as individual sacrifice for team success will stay together. Those kinds of families will not be pulled apart by selfishness. Philippians 2:3-4 says:

Let nothing be done through selfish ambition or conceit, but in lowliness of mind let each esteem others better than himself. Let each of you look out not only for his own interests, but also for the interests of others.

Yes, sacrificial living is Godly living.

The work place is another example of a team. People will produce so much more as they work together. The company will prosper when employers and employees are cooperating for a common purpose.

A church or civic organization is a team. People will achieve beyond the call of duty as they serve together. The organization will falter under selfish living. However, the organization will prosper from sacrificial service.

We could go on and on. Life is made up of many teams. In essence, we are all on one big team called humanity. All of civilization boils down to the ability to get along together. Let's face it; ultimately people who refuse to play team ball in society get locked up.

No one is an island completely unto themselves. Proverbs 18:1 says:

A man who isolates himself seeks his own desire; He rages against all wise judgment.

The Bible goes on to say in Proverbs 11:14:

Where there is no counsel, the people fall; But in the multitude of counselors there is safety.

Yes, the fool lives life totally for self. However, the wise person respects and values the input of others. No one has all the answers to every subject. We need each other.

Unfortunately, a team can become its own worst enemy. We have all seen very talented teams play like a group of individuals. The sad, but true, result is the simple fact that a united team of weaker talent will beat a talented group of individuals. Yes, players who work together will succeed. People of character understand that teamwork is: individual sacrifice for team success.

The story is told of game seven of the 1946 World Series. The St Louis Cardinals were matched up against the powerful Boston Red Sox. The Cardinals had been the underdog throughout the series, but had somehow managed to push the Red Sox into the seventh and deciding game.

In game five, Enos Slaughter, of the St Louis Cardinals, was hit on the elbow by a pitch. His arm began to hemorrhage and swelled up and the pain was agonizing. Slaughter continued on for two more innings like an "old warhorse." Finally, when he came up to bat again in the sixth inning, he did something for the first time in his career. He was unable to swing the bat or throw the ball, so he took himself out of the game.

The trainers worked on his arm, but nothing seemed to help. The next day he was taken to the team doctor for x-rays. He was given the devastating news to not play anymore in the World Series. The doctor warned Enos Slaughter that another injury could mean his arm would need to be amputated. Getting hit by a pitch or colliding with a player could ruin his career. The doctor said the risk of losing the arm was too great. He would have to wait until next season.

However, the Cardinals had tied the series in game six and now were ready for game seven. A World Series championship was on the line. The Cardinals needed Slaughter, but the doctors said the risk was too great.

However, Enos Slaughter defined "teamwork" as "individual sacrifice for team success." He showed up on "game day" wearing his uniform and insisted on playing. He begged the manager to ignore his injury and put him in the line up.

Well, Enos Slaughter took the field and was ready to give it his all. It was an incredible demonstration of will power and team spirit. The team had gone to war and Slaughter made sure the General was leading the way.

In the bottom of the eighth, Enos Slaughter came to bat. The score was tied 3-3. The pain in his arm was nearly unbearable. Enos Slaughter ignored the pain and stepped into the batters box like a mighty warrior. He got a base hit to start off the inning. The next two batters got out and Slaughter was still on first.

Now it was time for bravery and the stage was set for some heroics. Slaughter decided to steal second to get into position to score. He broke for second on the pitch, but the batter swung at the ball. Walker got a base hit and Slaughter was flying on the base pads. The center fielder took his time getting the ball as Slaughter rounded second and headed for third. The third base coach was holding Enos Slaughter at third. Therefore, the center fielder casually threw the ball to the cut off man.

However, Slaughter had been given permission in the dug out to take the plate anytime he thought he could make it. Therefore, he ignored the stop sign at third and raced for the plate. Enos Slaughter was literally risking his right arm for the team. A collision with the catcher could further damage his injured arm and require amputation.

Now with a World Series Championship at stake, Enos Slaughter put it all on the line for the team. He raced for home as he ran like a runaway locomotive. The throw was off the mark and Slaughter slid in safely for the go ahead run!

The Cardinals went on to win the game by the score of 4-3. They had miraculously won the 1946 World Series. It was the individual sacrifice of Enos Slaughter that brought team success. That is what teamwork is all about.

My friend, let me remind us of another individual sacrifice for team success. Two thousand years ago the Son of God made the greatest sacrifice of all time. Jesus Christ died on the cross for our sins. He rose again the third day proving that His sacrificial death gives us a victorious life.

God graciously invites us to join His team through faith in His Son. John 1:12 says:

> *But as many as received Him, to them He gave the right to become children of God, to those who believe in His name.*

Why not join God's team today. Tell God that you believe in the death, burial, and resurrection of Christ as the sacrifice for your sins. Through prayer, invite Christ into your life as your personal Lord & Savior and you will become a child of God. Simply trust in the individual sacrifice of Jesus and begin to experience the success God has for you on His team. After all, teamwork is individual sacrifice for team success.

CHAPTER 16

SELF CONTROL IS THE
SUCCESS OF WINNING THE BATTLE WITHIN

One very important ingredient to success is self-control. In actuality, self-control is the success of winning the battle within. Success or failure is often times determined by our victory or defeat over our attitude. As the saying goes: "Your attitude will determine your altitude."

Proverbs 16:32 says:

He who is slow to anger is better than the mighty, and he who rules his spirit than he who takes a city.

This is a powerful word picture. The Word of God is teaching the incredible power of ruling your inner spirit. True power is the championship character quality of self-control.

The picture is that of a mighty army that has surrounded a city. The powerful army will engage in great war tactics to gain the victory. The success will be a tremendous accomplishment and display of military force. The army that can overpower a fortified city is truly a powerful force to reckon with.

However, the person who can exercise self-control is more powerful than the mighty army. It includes the ability to control your emotions and master your inner spirit. Particularly when you gain the victory over your inner anger, you'll be on the march to success.

Perhaps you have heard the story of a young father who was pushing a baby carriage. He seemed to be unruffled by the screaming and bawling of the little baby. The young father simply whispered, "Easy Bobby. Keep calm now, Bobby." However, the baby just kept crying more loudly than ever. The young father simply responded, "Now, now, Bobby, don't lose your temper. It's okay. You'll be alright."

At that time, a compassionate grandmother walked over and gently picked up the crying baby. She tenderly calmed the baby and soothed the child's troubled spirit. She gently patted the baby and said to the child, "What's wrong Bobby? You'll be okay." The elderly woman also complimented the young father on his self-control. She said it was a beautiful sight to see him speaking so tenderly to the little baby named Bobby.

At that point, the father made an interesting point of clarification. First, he thanked the elderly woman for her loving care of the little baby. Then he told her that the baby's name was Johnny, and the fathers name was Bobby. Yes, it seems that the young father had been gently talking to himself in an effort to maintain proper self-control.

Yes, the one who rules his own spirit is truly better than the mighty! It may require a strong sense of discipline and willpower, but it will be worth the effort. In order to develop self-control, we must learn to guard our heart. Proverbs 4:23 says:

Keep your heart with all diligence, For out of it spring the issues of life.

Yes, we must learn to protect our heart from inner anger. The best way is to guard your heart against bitterness. It seems that the destructive flow of inner anger begins when bitterness takes root in our life.

Perhaps someone does you wrong. How will you respond? Will you harbor a grudge against that person? If so, the one you destroy may very well be yourself.

Perhaps someone mistreats a friend you love very dearly. They respond okay, but you may choose to take up an offense for them. Again, this will only destroy your inner peace as you take the bait of bitterness.

Sometimes you may become angry at the negative circumstances of life. Things just did not turn out as you expected. Now, you are faced with a choice. Will you allow inner anger to set in or will you trust the sovereign hand of God?

Philippians 2:13 says:

for it is God who works in you both to will and to do for His good pleasure.

That is exactly why Philippians 2:14 says:

Do all things without grumbling and complaining.

My friend, developing a confident trust in the sovereignty of God will give you a peace beyond human understanding. Instead of being torn apart by inner turmoil, you will have the sweet assurance that God is at work in your life.

Romans 8:28 says:

And we know that all things work together for good to those who love God, to those who are the called according to His purpose.

As your confidence in God continues to develop, you will learn to ask the right questions- such as: God, what do you want me to learn from this negative situation? God, how do you want to use this in my life to make me a better person? God, teach me to turn this negative situation into a positive experience of growth in my inner spirit. That type of attitude will guard your heart from negative and destructive forces.

A person of self-control will focus on the positive instead of the negative. Developing a positive disposition will help you navigate yourself in a positive direction. Your outlook will determine your outcome. Guarding your heart will guide your life. The Scripture says, "as a man thinks in his heart, so is he." Yes, self-control is directly related to your success.

A person of self-control will also have an inner spirit that reflects peace instead of poison. Notice the poisonous effect and explosive danger of bitterness. Ephesians 4:31 says:

Let all bitterness, wrath, anger, clamor, and evil speaking be out away from you, with all malice.

Now, notice that forgiveness is the best way to combat bitterness. Ephesians 4:32 says:

And be kind to one another, tenderhearted, forgiving one another, just as God in Christ also forgave you.

Yes, a person of self-control will be a forgiving person. This will keep you from having inner anger swell up within and explode without.

I'm reminded of growing up and watching my mom can green beans. Mom was an incredible cook and she preferred "homemade" food instead of "store bought." Each summer we would plant a huge garden. We enjoyed fresh vegetables all summer and Mom would can them for the winter, as well. It certainly helped to stretch the budget, but most importantly, it added great flavor to her cooking.

I can still taste my mom's homemade vegetable soup. It was fantastic! I can remember coming home from school and smelling the soup simmering on the stove. As soon as you walked into the house, you were struck with the "sweet smelling aroma." It makes my mouth water just thinking about it.

Mom also had a special way of cooking green beans, which were my favorite vegetable. Mom would fry a few strips of bacon and cook the green beans in the grease for flavor. I loved it and always ate my fair share. In fact, Mom would often times make an extra quart of green beans if I was going to be home for supper. I could literally make a meal out of them.

Consequently, Mom would always can plenty of green beans. One summer day, Mom put a batch of green beans into the Mason jars for canning. She put the quart jars into the pressure cooker and placed them on the stove in the basement. That is when the excitement was about to begin.

Later that evening, we were watching TV in the living room. All of a sudden, we heard a very loud explosion! It sounded like someone had fired a rifle in the basement! That is when we remembered the green beans in the pressure cooker on the basement stove.

We went downstairs and found an enormous mess. Green beans and broken glass were all over the place. The steam had not been released from the pressure cooker. Eventually, it exploded! It was certainly a night to remember!

In a similar way, that is what happens to us when we refuse to forgive people. The "steam" of our grudge and inner anger builds "pressure" in our heart. Eventually, there is a destructive explosion. Therefore, to avoid such damaging results, it is much better to "release the steam" and choose to forgive those who wrong us. This will allow you the power to demonstrate the positive quality of self-control.

Yes, self-control is necessary to win the battle within. "He who rules his spirit is truly better than the mighty."

My friend, look to Jesus for the strength you need for self-control. Trust in His death, burial and resurrection for your forgiveness of sins. Follow Christ by faith and you will experience the success of self-control and you will win the battle within.

CHAPTER 17

PERSEVERANCE IS
YOUR GOLD MINE TO SUCCESS

Perseverance—the ability to persist and hold on during any endeavor. Hanging in there while pursuing a goal with the refusal to throw in the towel. The removal of the word "quit" from your vocabulary.

Franklin Roosevelt said: "When you come to the end of your rope, tie a knot, and hang on."

Vince Lombardi said this: "It is not whether you get knocked down, it is whether you get up."

Another great leader said this about perseverance: "You do not determine the greatness of an individual by their talent or wealth, but rather by what it takes to discourage them."

Remember, perseverance is your gold mine to success. Jesus said in Luke 9:62: "No one, having put his hand to the plow, and looking back, is fit for the kingdom of God." Yes, in our service and dedication to the Lord, the only direction is "forward."

Do not entertain thoughts of doubt concerning the importance of your dedication to God. My friend, your life is important to God. You have a divine destiny to fulfill and God will empower you to serve Him. God will give you a sense of mission and purpose, regardless of your age, financial status, or educational background. God has a plan for your life.

The important thing for you to do is faithfully live for Him. The Scripture says in Galatians 6:9:

And let us not grow weary while doing good, for in due season we shall reap if we do not lose heart.

Yes, your life will have a positive impact on others. Hang in there and always hope for the best. Discover your sense of mission and then pursue it with all your heart. Dedicate your energy to a meaningful purpose and endure the worst as you expect the best.

Calvin Coolidge said: "Press on. Nothing in the world can take the place of persistence. Talent will not; nothing is more common than unsuccessful men with talent. Genius will not; unrewarded genius is almost a proverb. Education alone will not; the world is full of educated derelicts. Persistence and determination alone are omnipotent."

Yes my friend, there is no substitute for persistence. So often the fine line between success and failure is found in one word, "Perseverance." The ability to hang on. The determination to dig in your heels and refuse to give up.

The greatest motivation to keep on keeping on is faith in the risen Lord. We can rest assured that God has provided humanity with the answer to our greatest need. Jesus died and rose again for our sins. God offers us a relationship with Him by faith. Once we trust in Jesus as our Savior, we come into fellowship with God. This guarantees we are on the winning team.

The Bible says in I Corinthians 15:57 -

But thanks be to God, who gives us the victory through our Lord Jesus Christ.

Yes, there is victory in Jesus. There is hope for any situation. There is power for living in Jesus Christ. Once we anchor our faith in Christ, we can rest assured that our life will be triumphant. We will be used of God for His glory. We can serve Him with gladness.

The Scripture says in I Corinthians 15:58:

Therefore, my beloved brethren, be steadfast, immovable, always abounding in the work of the Lord, knowing that your labor is not in vain in the Lord.

Yes, faith in Christ is your ultimate power to persevere. You can be fully confident that your service to the Lord will always be the right thing to do. You cannot go wrong in following Jesus. He will be your Savior, Lord, and the friend who sticks closer than a brother. He will empower you with perseverance, which will become your gold mine to success.

I'm reminded of a story of the California Gold Rush. It seems that two brothers sold all they had and moved west. They decided to try their hand at prospecting for gold. They bought the supplies necessary and began to search for gold.

Eventually, they discovered a beautiful sight in the ground. They had uncovered a vein of the shining gold ore. They staked their claim and began to mine the gold with great enthusiasm.

Unfortunately, the gold ran out in just a short time. It seemed they had only discovered a small vein of gold in the earth. Their pot of gold at the end of the rainbow was destined to be a small one. Finally, they gave up in disgust.

Consequently, the brothers found a buyer for their equipment and sold it all. They also sold their rights to the claim for a few hundred dollars. They decided they were not meant to be rich millionaires. The brothers were pleased with the small amount of gold they had found, but wished it could have been more. Oh, they had made some money, but had not struck it rich by any means.

Their "gold fever" had come and gone. They gave up and took the train back home. They had spent enough of their valuable time searching California for the valuable gold.

However, the man who bought their claim decided to keep pursuing the gold. He hired an engineer to examine the ground where the brothers had been mining. The engineer surveyed the ground and gave some very interesting advice. He instructed the new owner to continue digging in the exact same spot where the former owners had left off.

The man began to dig a little deeper. To the new owners amazement, he struck gold just three feet below where the brothers had quit. In fact, he struck a huge vein that was worth millions. The gold was mined and the new owner was a huge success.

Think about it. Had the two brothers used just a little more persistence, they would have been rich. They would have been wealthy millionaires if they have only persevered. Just a little more work would have brought an enormous amount of success.

My friend, perseverance is your gold mine to success. Never, never, never quit. You may be so much closer to success than you can imagine. Always hang in there and refuse to give up. God promises that we will reap if we do not lose heart. Keep your eyes focused on God and your heart will have the strength to go on. Depend on God for your perseverance and you will strike your gold mine to success.

CHAPTER 18

SUCCESS HAS NO SHORTCUTS

I want to consider a very important character quality. It is a key ingredient to being successful in any occupation. It is good old fashioned, common everyday, hard work. That's right, working hard and developing a great work ethic is central to success. The hard worker knows that success has no shortcuts.

The book of Proverbs says this in 13:4:

The soul of a sluggard desires, and has nothing, but the soul of the diligent shall be made rich.

In other words, lazy people want things, but lack the will to work for them. Successful people, on the other hand, learn to discipline themselves to work hard. The natural result is the reward of getting ahead in life.

Vince Lombardi said this: "The harder you work, the harder it is to surrender." Lombardi also said "The dictionary is the only place that success comes before work." Yes, hard work and success go hand in hand.

It has been said that the path of least resistance often leads to nowhere. My friend, the easiest way is not necessarily the best way. People who look for the easiest road in life often wind up on a dead-end street.I firmly believe that God blesses the hard worker. Proverbs 10:4 says:

He who deals with a slack hand becomes poor, but the hand of the diligent becomes rich.

In other words, if you are lazy you will short change yourself. However, if you work hard, you will experience the sweet satisfaction of success.

Many people develop an unhealthy attitude of expectancy. People often act like the government owes them a living. We need to remember that we have the right to pursue happiness. This means we can work hard and create an opportunity. It has been rightly said that success comes when preparation meets opportunity.

Proverbs 21:5 says:

The plans of the diligent lead surely to plenty, but those of everyone who is hasty, surely to poverty.

In other words, successful people work hard and think things through. They don't make quick decisions that will be regretted later on.

Let's review the principles of success we have learned today from the book of Proverbs. We are to work hard (the hand of the diligent makes one rich. Proverbs 10:4). We are to be disciplined and have the will power to achieve (the soul of the diligent will be made rich. Proverbs 13:4). We are to make our plans wisely (the plans of the diligent lead surely to plenty. Proverbs 21:5). In other words: Success Has No Shortcuts.

Carefully consider Proverbs 21:6:

Getting treasures by a lying tongue is the fleeting fantasy of those who seek death.

In other words, those who lack character and lie, cheat, or steal to get ahead, wind up destroying themselves. Eventually, those who try to succeed by short cutting their character will fail in the long run.

Genuinely successful people have goals that go beyond the dollar bill. Truly successful people emphasize family values and the work ethic. Money is not their biggest motivating factor. It is their sense of responsibility in meeting the needs of their family. They have the core values of hard work, discipline and responsible living. Their happiness is the result of balance in life and the satisfaction of caring for their family. True success has no shortcuts.

Remember, character is what you are; it is not what you possess. Develop the character quality of hard work, and success will take care of itself. Find something worthwhile and throw your whole life into it. Colossians 3:23 says:

And whatever you do, do it heartily, as to the Lord and not to men.

Yes, put your heart into your work. Give it everything you've got. Be willing to go the extra mile. After all, extra ordinary effort may make the little difference for incredible success.

When you think about it, there is a fine line between being good and great. However, the payoff can be phenomenal. The athlete who puts in that little something extra may receive tremendous dividends. The same is true in business as well. You can apply the principle of hard work to any area of your life. My friend, as you work hard and pursue your dreams, you will achieve greatness. The sky is the limit for the one who is willing to reach for the stars.

However, this is where spiritual guidance is so crucial. You want to make sure you are pursuing the plans God has for you. After all, as you climb the ladder of success, you will want to be sure it is leaning against the right wall.

That's where the Word of God will protect you. Joshua 1:8 says:

This Book of the Law shall not depart from your mouth, but you shall meditate in it day and night, that you may observe to do according to all that is written in it. For then you will make your way prosperous, and then you will have good success.

Yes, God will guide your path of success as you follow His Word. He will make sure your ladder of success is leaning against the right wall.

You know, when I consider the truth: Success has no shortcuts; I'm reminded of the great boxer, Rocky Marciano. Early in his amateur career, his arms would get tired after just a couple of rounds. In fact, he could barely hold his arms up after just a few rounds.

Of course, as his arms would begin to sag to his side, it was disastrous. He would take a terrible beating from his sparring partners. With this glaring weakness, few gave Marciano much hope of becoming a champion.

However, Rocky Marciano was determined to work hard for success. He began going to the local YMCA swimming pool to work out. He developed a creative way to strengthen his arms. He would submerge himself in the water and practice punching under water. He would swing his arms wildly against the water.

He would practice his punching with his arms under water for hours on end. He did this day after day for several months. Eventually, he was strong enough to begin his professional career.

When Rocky Marciano retired, he was undefeated as a pro boxer. He won all 49 of his professional fights, and 45 were by knock out punches. He was the world champion and one of the greatest boxers in the history of the sport.

However, his success did not come easy. He worked for it. In fact, you could say that he spelled "talent" W-O-R-K. After all, Success has no shortcuts.

My friend, spiritual success has no shortcuts as well. It cost Jesus Christ His life. He died on the cross for our sins and rose again. Jesus offers us the free gift of eternal life when we invite Christ into our life by faith. While the grace of God is free, it is not cheap. It cost Jesus Christ everything. Yes, Jesus took no shortcuts on His journey to the cross.

Therefore, we can thank Jesus for setting the ultimate example that: True success has no shortcuts.

CHAPTER 19

ENCOURAGEMENT IS
THE PARTNER OF SUCCESS

I fully believe that encouragement is the partner of success. After all, encouragement will always cheer you on with hope. As you know, hope will inspire success. Therefore, encouragement is the partner of success.

Let's face it. We all need encouragement. To encourage someone is to build courage into their heart. A positive word of affirmation can go a long way to encourage someone.

Proverbs 12:25 says:

Anxiety in the heart of man causes depression, But a good word makes it glad.

Yes, sometimes the anxiety of life can weigh someone down. It can lead to a spirit of depression. The world that once appeared bright and sunny may now look dark and gloomy.

Yet, in the midst of despair, a simple word of encouragement can lift someone's spirit. Your kind word may be the gentle touch their inner spirit is longing for. God will use your positive words of affirmation to be an inspiration to the down-hearted.

When you consider home and family life, God often uses the mother as an encourager. In many homes, mom is the one who provides the loving affirmation. Mom is the one who says a kind word at just the right moment. Mom will be the one to provide the gentle encouragement to pick up the family.

Proverbs 18:21-22 says:

Death and life are in the power of the tongue, and those who love it will eat its fruit. He who finds a wife finds a good thing, and obtains favor from the Lord.

The Lord has smiled upon the home that is blessed with a godly woman who speaks kind works of loving affirmation. I certainly thank God for my wife, Cindi. She is a tremendous encourager and my partner of success. I believe her legacy will be passed on through our daughter, Hannah, who is growing into a godly young lady as well. Hannah has a sweet spirit, like her mother, and I am confident that God will prepare her to become someone's partner of success.

Yes, success will be found in the family that encourages one another. Confidence will blossom when encouragement is allowed to flourish. Encouragement is truly the partner of success.

Friendships that are healthy will focus on encouragement. Proverbs 27:17 says:

As iron sharpens iron, so a man sharpens the countenance of his friend.

Yes, a positive friendship will build each other up. A positive friendship will look for the best in one another. A positive friendship will strengthen each other with encouragement. Others will be enriched when you seek to be an encouragement. You will be the type of person that others enjoy being around. You will lift up the spirit in people and become a positive friend.

My friend, all relationships flourish in an atmosphere of encouragement. In fact, the Bible instructs Christians to be an encouragement to one another. Hebrews 10:24-25 says:

And let us consider one another in order to stir up love and good works, not forsaking the assembling of ourselves together, as is the manner of some, but exhorting one another, and so much the more as you see the Day approaching.

Yes, believers in Christ are to gather together for the purpose of mutual encouragement. This will refresh the heart of the believer. It will recharge the spiritual battery, so to speak.

That's why the Christian home is to be a place of encouragement. People in the family ought to look forward to being together. Spending quality time together as a family will be a joy when encouragement is present. The family that encourages one another will be a family that enjoys one another.

Jesus said in John 13:34-35:

A new commandment I give to you, that you love one another; as I have loved you, that you also love one another. By this all will know that you are My disciples, if you have love for one another.

Yes, the love that flows from the heart of Jesus to the heart of believers will be a dynamic witness for Christ. Others will see your faith in God and your love for each other. You will display a Power for Living that will be a contagious form of positive Christianity.

The encouragement that others receive from your positive outlook on life will be an inspiration. Your attitude will help others soar to a new altitude. Your encouragement will be someone's partner in success.

Years ago, a little boy came home from school with a note from his teacher. The boy's mother opened the letter and read the note. The mother was appalled at the note from the teacher.

It seems that the teacher had met with the school officials concerning the capabilities of this particular student. Together, the school officials decided the boy should be removed from school. They decided that the partially deaf boy was too stupid to learn.

The mother read the note and became outraged. She proclaimed, "My son Tom, is not too stupid to learn. Why, I'll teach him myself."

From that point on the mother worked with her little son named Tom. She helped her partially deaf son learn to read and write. She taught him math and science. My, how her son Tom, loved science. He would attack the subject with a passion.

Tom took to science like a fish to water. He seemed to find his mission for life. He allowed his creative mind to flow. His passion for science was driven by his desire to create. All along, his mother just kept encouraging him to pursue his dreams.

Tom kept learning and developing. Eventually, he proved how wrong the school officials were. After all, Thomas Edison was by no means too stupid to learn!

As you know, Thomas Edison went on to invent the light bulb. In fact, when he died, the people of the United States of America paid an incredible tribute to him. They turned off the nations lights for one full minute. It reminded the people what life would be like without the light Thomas Edison had created. Of course, he also invented the motion picture and record player. All in all, Thomas Edison had more than 1000 patents to his name.

Yes, encouragement is the partner of success. Where would this world be if Thomas Edison's mother had accepted the opinion of the school authorities? How fortunate we are that she chose to be an encouragement to her son. The world is truly a better place because of the encouragement of one mother to her son.

By the way, just as Thomas Edison turned on the lights for the world, the Word of God will turn on the light of Jesus. 2000 years ago the Lord Jesus Christ demonstrated the love of God by dying on the cross for our sins. He rose again the third day proving His victory over the grave.

Today, He offers the free gift of eternal life to anyone who will trust in Christ. The gift of eternal life is the ultimate example of love and encouragement for humanity. God will give you spiritual success through faith in Jesus.

Reach out to Jesus and discover that His encouragement will be your partner of success.

CHAPTER 20

SUCCESS COMES WHEN
PREPARATION MEETS OPPORTUNITY

It has been said that "you cannot climb the ladder of success with your hands in your pockets." In other words, be the kind of person that takes initiative. Don't wait for life to come to you, go out and make it happen. Don't wait for your ship to come in, swim out and get it.

Abraham Lincoln said: "I will prepare and someday my chance will come." Well, Abraham Lincoln did not stumble upon the office of President of the United States. No, he understood that: "Success comes when preparation meets opportunity."

My friend, I want to encourage you to make the most of your God-given potential. Capitalize on the opportunities that God offers you. After all, your greatest responsibility to God is to be faithful to fulfill your God-given potential.

You know, God is not nearly as interested in your ability as He is your availability. God is not necessarily looking for talent, but He is looking for people who will be trustworthy to Him. After all, God is the one who bestows people with their talent. Therefore, God simply wants you to be faithful with your life in service to God.

As you live a life of faithfulness to God, you will learn to "seize the moment" that God gives you. You will be ready when the time is right. You will discover the success God has designed for you. Yes, your God-given success will come when your preparation meets your God-given opportunity.

Jesus taught this important principle in His "Parable of the Talents." The Scripture says in Matthew 25:14-18:

For the kingdom of heaven is like a man traveling to a far country, who called his own servants and delivered his goods to them. And to one he gave five talents, to another two, and to another one, to each according to his own ability; and immediately he went on a journey. Then he who had received the five talents went and traded with them, and made another five talents. And likewise he who had received two gained two more also. But he who had received one went and dug in the ground, and hid his lord's money.

Jesus told the story of three men who were given various God-given opportunities. Two of three capitalized on their God-given potential and achieved great success. However, one ignored his God-given opportunity. Consequently, his life did not fulfill the greatest possible potential. As a result, he did not live up to the expectation level and was a disappointment to God and a disgrace to himself.

Keep in mind this story is a parable told by our Lord. A parable is an earthly story with a heavenly meaning. This is not a story on "money management." God simply uses the illustration of managing money to teach the principle of being faithful to the Lord with our God-given potential.

Each of the three people received an endowment from the Lord. They were all given talents ranging from one to five in number. A talent was a large piece of silver that weighed between 58-80 pounds. As you can see, a talent was a significant amount of money in those days. In fact, a talent represented 20 years of wages for the average worker.

Consequently, this was sure to get the attention of the listeners. After all, this was no small chunk of change that Jesus gave out. However, the important principle to keep in mind is what the talents represented. You see the talents were symbolic of opportunities God gave to each one.

It's also interesting to note that the Lord gave different opportunities to different people. Some were given five talents, some two, and some only one. The importance is not the amount of talents God gave. No, the true significance is the expectation the Lord gave was the same for everyone. He simply required the people to be faithful with their God-given opportunities.

Basically, each one was expected to do something with what God had given them. Their opportunity had come and they were expected to be prepared for it. The ladder of success had been placed on the wall in front of them and now they were expected to climb as far as God would allow.

In fact, the major expectation was to faithfully fulfill their God-given opportunities. They were not held accountable for talents they were not given. They were simply expected to be responsible with the talents they were given.

God expected them to multiply their life and achieve their maximum potential. We can even notice that the same reward was given to the one who turned five talents into ten and the one who expanded two talents into four. Both were told, "Well done my good and faithful servant."

The only one who was punished was the individual who buried his talent. God fully expected Him to do something with his life, but he wasted it. The one who buried his talent was motivated by fear and not faith. It was fear and insecurity that kept him from taking a chance. Fear of failure caused him to be frozen in a state of mediocrity.

Faith set the other two free to succeed. Faith enabled them to double their assets and achieve as God designed. However, fear kept the other from doing anything with his opportunity. The sad reality is the fact that he also lost the very thing he tried to hang on to.

As the old saying goes: "Use it or lose it." He buried his talent and God took it away from him. Isn't it true that fear causes people to look at what they might lose instead of what could be gained? The result is that you often times lose it anyway. It is simply a slower death. Nothing can be sadder in life than to look back at the missed opportunities.

However, the life of faith looks to the future with optimism. The positive minded person capitalizes on opportunities and lives life to the fullest. They also experience the rich reward of the blessing of God. The life of faith is filled with sweet satisfaction.

You know, I'm reminded of the story of the time the famous composer, Ignace Jan Paderewski was scheduled to give a concert. It was an evening to remember as the people came to observe the great Paderewski. The men wore black tuxedos and the women were dressed in beautiful evening gowns. It was a prestigious gathering to say the least.

The crowd sat in great anticipation as they waited for Paderewski to make his way to the stage. Meanwhile, a little boy sat with his mother. However, sitting still was very difficult for this highly energetic boy of nine years of age. The mother turned her head for a moment and her nine year old son was gone. To her surprise he made his way to the stage. The beautiful Steinway piano had caught his eye. To the shock of the entire crowd, the little boy began to play "chopsticks."

The crowd began to shout for the boy to be removed from the piano. The crowd shouted, "Where are his parents?" They cried out for the boy to be taken away from the piano. The scene was quickly becoming ugly. However, the little boy just kept right on playing "chopsticks."

Meanwhile, Paderewski heard the roar of the crowd and quickly made his way to the stage. However, he did not stop the boy from playing. In fact, he stepped up behind the boy and leaned over and started playing a countermelody with the child. He whispered for the boy to keep playing and not to quit. Paderewski improvised beautifully and together the song sounded incredible. The audience was delighted as such a simple song could be transformed into a beautiful melody.

The crowd cheered when the famous composer added his personal touches to the simple song of chopsticks. It became a beautiful work of art as the master performer added his hand of blessing.

My friend, you may feel like your life is as simple as chopsticks. However, as you faithfully serve the Lord with the talent he has given you, God will turn your life into a beautiful symphony. Remember, success comes when preparation meets opportunity.

CHAPTER 21

SUCCESSFUL PEOPLE STRETCH WITH CHALLENGES, UNSUCCESSFUL PEOPLE SHRINK FROM CHALLENGES

One trademark of successful people is their desire to face a challenge. The mindset of success will stretch with challenges. Successful people learn to welcome challenges because they know it will bring improvement. Consequently, successful people learn to meet a challenge head on. Yes, successful people stretch with challenges, unsuccessful people shrink from challenges.

The thrill of facing a challenge motivates the successful person from within. Their heart yearns for the next mountain to climb. They live by the peak-to-peek principle. In other words, they climb one mountain peak and are now able to see the next one. Their life is constantly growing and evolving.

In a spiritual realm, verses like Matthew 19:26 are at the core of their being. Jesus said:

with men this is impossible, but with God, all things are possible.

The excitement of accomplishing great things through the power of God brings tremendous enthusiasm.

Successful people have removed the word "impossible" from their vocabulary. After all, Jesus also said in Mark 9:23:

If you can believe, all things are possible to him who believes.

Successful people in the kingdom of God have learned to overcome their fears by the power of faith. Their focus is on the strength of their God, and not the size of their challenge. You see my friend, successful people stretch with a challenge. They have the faith to believe that: "Today's problems will groom them for tomorrow's potential."

However, the unsuccessful person will shrink away from a challenge. They have a fear-based mentality. Their goal is not to succeed in life. No, their goal is simply to survive in life.

The idea of stretching to meet a challenge brings a "fear based anxiety." Unsuccessful people will sacrifice the opportunities for personal growth in order to maintain personal security. They often will shrink away from a path that has a few problems. However, the path of least resistance often leads to nowhere.

You see my friend; God often uses the problems of life to mold our character. God is the potter and we are the clay. The challenges of life will make the clay soft and pliable in the hands of the potter. God will use the challenges of life to shape us to further resemble the Savior.

God will use the difficult experiences of life to deepen our faith. In fact, as we learn to walk with God and face the challenge, we will learn to welcome the next challenge. This is the result of the exciting experience of learning the faithfulness of God and the power of His Word.

We have the opportunity to apply such powerful verses of scripture like II Timothy 1:7, which says:

For God has not given us a spirit of fear, but of power and of love and of a sound mind.

Yes, God wants us to move forward by faith, not shrink back in fear. After all, God does not abandon His children on this earth. In fact, the Christian faith gives the believer the power of God to achieve success that is motivated by love for God.

Yes, the Christian life is the ultimate level of living. The believer actually has the Holy Spirit of God living inside you. That's why Romans 8:31 says:

What then shall we say to these things? If God is for us, who can be against us?

My friend, do not let the devil rob you of your zest for living. John 10:10 says:

The thief does not come except to steal, and to kill, and to destroy. I have come that they may have life, and that they may have it more abundantly.

Yes, Satan would love to get you to focus on the negative. He delights in robbing you of your joy. His goal is to draw your attention onto life's problems. He wants to bring discouragement to your inner spirit and destruction to your positive spirit.

However, Jesus has a much better plan. Jesus offers you the abundant life. This is the highest quality of life available. He will focus your mind on God's solutions to meet any challenge. Jesus will empower you to rise above your problems and live on the mountaintop.

Jesus will enable you to pursue your God-given potential. He will give you the faith to establish your goals. He will help you "climb every mountain until you find your dream." Jesus will give you a life of satisfaction and fulfillment.

Yes, my friend, successful people stretch with challenges. They know the value of a life of vision. They live by faith, which will improve their sight of God. This will further develop their security in God.

However, unsuccessful people shrink from challenges. Fear of failure causes them to pull back. Mediocrity becomes their way of life. It's a sad state of being. It is sad because they cannot see themselves in the light of God's power. They would rather cling to the comfortable. Sadly enough, they miss the thrill of tackling the impossible.

You know, the Bible is full of stories of ordinary people who achieved extra ordinary success. The common theme is their faith in the power of God.

One of my favorite examples is the story of Peter stepping out of the boat and joining the Lord on top of the water. You can read about it in Matthew 14:22-33.

Jesus had just fed the 5000 with five loaves of bread and two fish. He demonstrated His miracle working power by multiplying the small amount of food to feed a large amount of people. Now He has sent the disciples in a boat to cross the Sea of Galilee. Meanwhile, Christ has gone off to pray. However, during the middle of the night a storm arose. The disciples were in the middle of the Sea of Galilee and in the heart of the storm.

Sometime between 3:00 and 6:00am, the Lord came walking on the water. Obviously, it scared the disciples to death. The scripture says they "cried out for fear." However, Jesus immediately spoke to the disciples and calmed their fears. He said; "Be of good cheer, It is I, do not be afraid."

Well, Peter became pretty excited by the historic moment. After all, there was his Lord walking on the water toward their boat! Peter gets pretty wound up and decides he would like to get in on the action.

Now keep in mind for a moment, Peter was a fisherman by trade. He was just a common man from a common home. He had grown up working in the family business. They had been out on the Sea of Galilee countless times before. No doubt he had faced various storms before. So the fact that he was frightened tells us this was a serious storm. After all, Peter was very experienced in handling a boat.

Peter was also fully aware that walking on top of the water was humanly impossible. Yet, there was His Lord strolling on the stormy seas. Peter knew this was a moment of a lifetime. This was his one great opportunity to experience the impossible. This was his big chance to overcome every possible obstacle. His faith could shine brightly.

Peter asks permission to join the Lord in His walk on the water. Jesus extends the invitation for Peter to join Christ in this monumental moment. Peter gets out of the boat and is walking on the water himself. His eyes are fixed on Christ and he is experiencing the power of God. The thought that "with God all things are possible" was probably racing through the mind of Peter. He had seized the moment and was experiencing a miracle of faith.

For a brief moment in time, Peter was on top of the world. He was achieving what no other human being had ever done before. Peter was walking on the water with Christ!

Every other disciple could only watch in amazement. Peter was leading the way for great success. He had stretched his faith to meet the challenge. He had conquered an incredible obstacle through faith in Christ. I realize that Peter eventually looked at the storm and started to sink. However, let's give him a little credit. After all, eleven others were still sitting in the boat! Peter had stepped out on faith and had literally walked on water. Peter also had enough sense to cry out to the Lord when his faith wavered.

Peter cried out: "Lord save me." The Lord Jesus immediately stretched out His hand and caught him. By the way, Jesus still does the same today. He saves all who call upon Him in faith believing. The Lord is rich in mercy to all who call upon Him.

Remember my friend, even with small faith, Peter walked on water. Think of what you can do through the power of God. Keep your eyes on Christ and stretch for success.

Never forget, successful people stretch with challenges, while unsuccessful people shrink from challenges.

CHAPTER 22

THERE IS ONE TIME
WHEN LOSING IS WINNING

Everybody loves a winner! People love to jump on the bandwagon and support a winner. In fact, we even have a name for the "bandwagon followers." We call them "fair weather fans."

A "fair weather fan" is someone who comes around when a team is on a winning streak. They will cheer wildly as long as the team is winning. However, when the team losses begin to mount up, the "fair weather fan" is nowhere to be found.

The point is: we all love a winner. General Patton once said: "Americans love a winner and will not tolerate a loser." Vince Lombardi said: "If you can accept losing, you cannot win." General Douglas McArthur said: "In war, there is no substitute for victory."

These types of statements pretty much sum up the way most competitors feel about winning. A true competitor has that fire in their spirit that longs for victory. Their heart beats a little faster at the thought of winning and their stomach turns at the idea of losing. The thirst in their soul can only be quenched with a championship. V-I-C-T-O-R-Y - that is the competitors only battle cry!

Yes, whether it is a child at the little league diamond or an adult at the corporate headquarters: People want to win. It is the thrill of victory that we strive to experience.

However, there is one time when losing is winning. Jesus said that if we follow Him completely; we will have to give some things up in order to gain the richest possession. Luke 9:23-25 says:

Then He said to them all, 'If anyone desires to come after Me, let him deny himself, and take up his cross daily, and follow Me. For whoever desires to save his life will lose it, but whoever loses his life for My sake will save it. For what profit is it to a man if he gains the whole world, and is himself destroyed or lost?'

In this passage of Scripture, Jesus is teaching a concept of true fulfillment. It's interesting to note that the teaching of Jesus "flies in the face" of modern culture. We seem to live in the "me generation." The most important principle is to "look out for number one."

However, Jesus confronts this idea of self-satisfaction. Jesus is teaching the importance of self-sacrifice and self-denial. Jesus is actually proclaiming the importance of laying down our personal rights.

In fact, Jesus is teaching His followers to lose in order to win. The follower of Christ must lose the battle of self-fulfillment in order to win the value of "Kingdom Living." Jesus is calling for His disciples to be fully surrendered followers of Christ. This will enable Christians to experience the joy of a Christ centered life.

In order to lose to win, we must live a life of complete surrender to Christ. The entire Christian faith is centered around following Jesus Christ. He becomes the Lord and Master of the Christian. Our relationship with Christ must have priority above all other relationships. Jesus is Lord and he expects to rule our life. We are to surrender our will to Him. We are to deny our own personal desires and seek to please the Lord.

In this process, Jesus will reward our life with true soul satisfaction. We will enter a level of living that is above our selfish nature. We will travel the high road of success as we humbly serve Christ.

This act of surrender to the Lord is like putting a new driver at the wheel. We give Jesus the steering wheel of our life and allow Him to direct our decisions. We turn over to the Lord the reigns of our life. We allow Christ to have complete control of the decision making process. We allow His Word to govern our actions. The good news is found in the fact that His Word is the "truth that will set you free." Consequently, as the Scripture says: "When the Son of God sets you free, you will be free indeed."

You see my friend; the self-centered person lives a shallow life. When you are the center of your world you may discover that: "It's a small world after all." Jesus said we are to "take up our cross daily." This gives us the idea of sacrifice. Yes, in order to lose to win, we must also be willing to sacrifice.

In Roman times, the cross was symbolic of death. It was always a public execution when someone was crucified. In fact, the person would carry their own crossbeam to their crucifixion. All personal rights were gone and all hope was lost. It was a total surrender to Roman Law and the sacrifice of one's life.

Therefore, when Jesus tells us to take up our cross and follow Him, Jesus is teaching us to surrender to His Word and sacrifice our life in service to Him. Jesus is calling us to a life of dedication to the will of God.

However, it is not a life of ruin. It is a life of reward. Jesus promises to bless His followers with a meaningful life. Once you give your life to Christ, He will give it back to you with a new perspective. You will learn to give up the temporary and live for the eternal. The result will be the rich reward of the inner peace and sweet satisfaction that only Christ can give to you.

You know, when you think of winning, you have to consider the great dynasties of the New York Yankees. Through the years they have certainly had some of the greatest players and teams of all times. Just mentioning a few "Yankee greats" like Babe Ruth, Lou Gerrig, Joe DiMaggio, Mickey Mantle, Roger Maris, Yogi Berra, and you think of World Series Championships. However, one former "Yankee great" shocked major league baseball when he retired at the peak of his career. His name was Bobby Richardson.

Bobby was a seven time all star and a five time golden glove winner. He played second base for the 1961 Yankees that were considered the greatest baseball team of all time. He was no stranger to World Series Championships while playing for the great New York Yankees.

He was the most valuable player of the 1960 World Series, even though the Yankees lost to the Pittsburgh Pirates. In 1962, he led the American League with 209 base hits.

Bobby was truly a great player on a great team. He was in a position that many people would have envied, to say the least. He was a star player on a winning dynasty. Yet, in 1966, at the age of 31, at the height of his career, he retired from baseball. The Yankee owner tried to talk him out of it. The owner offered Richardson a blank contract and told Bobby to fill in the amount of his own salary.

However, Bobby Richardson told the Yankee owner that it was not about money. His decision was based on family values. He wanted to spend more time with his family. Consequently, he walked away from his incredible opportunity with the New York Yankees.

You see, Bobby is a Christian and he felt the Lord wanted him off the road and home with his family. He turned down fortune and fame to dedicate his time to his family. He wanted to be there while his children were growing up.

The result: Well, along with the wonderful opportunity to be a loving husband and father, Bobby shared many special times with his family. He was able to pass on the Christian faith to his children. In fact, two of his sons went on to be ministers of the gospel.

Bobby has been used of the Lord in a mighty way. He was even given the privilege of visiting Mickey Mantle on his deathbed. At Mantle's request, Bobby Richardson was able to lead Mickey Mantle to faith in Jesus Christ.

My friend, there is one time when losing is winning. That is when you give up personal ambition and follow the Lord with complete devotion. Losing your life in service to Christ is winning in this life and the life to come.

CHAPTER 23

FAITH PURSUES YOUR DREAM

It has been said that "daring to dream is daring to live." Yes, there is power in pursuing your dream. In fact, no one is old who refuses to give up their dream. Faith pursues your dream. Bold faith paves the way for bountiful living.

The Psalmist said in Psalm 27:13-14:

I would have lost heart, unless I had believed that I would see the goodness of the Lord in the land of the living. Wait on the Lord; Be of good courage, and He shall strengthen your heart; Wait, I say, on the Lord!

You see my friend; no one loses heart with their mind focused on a positive faith. The simple reason is positive faith produces powerful living. Positive faith says that God's goodness will shine upon me. I will experience God's greatness and His goodness in the here and now. I will stay motivated as I wait on the Lord.

This type of faith goes after the future with courage from the Lord. The strong heart filled with bold courage will have the faith to pursue your dream. Walt Disney said, "If you can dream it, you can do it, after all, this whole thing got started by a mouse."

In fact, let's consider the amazing story of Walt Disney. At the age of 17, young Walt was a bottle washer and an apple masher at a jelly factory in Chicago. His dad was the supervisor and helped him land a job with security.

However, Walt Disney's dreams were bigger than working in the jelly factory. So, in the year of 1919, at the age of 17, he moved to Kansas City in search for work to apply his skills as an artist. The idea of drawing for a living appealed to him so off he went to pursue his dream.

His first job was that of an apprentice to help draw farm equipment ads. This lasted for two months, during October and November. Once the pre-holiday rush was taken care of, the job was eliminated and Walt Disney was let go.

A short time later, he landed a job with the Kansas City Film Ad Company. This job consisted of making 60 second animated cartoon movies to be shown as commercials in the local movie houses. Cardboard cutouts were used instead of drawings.

However, Disney had a desire to improve upon the process. He persuaded his boss to lend him a camera and Walt began moonlighting in the evenings. His experimentation and determination helped him improve the animated process.

Soon he produced brief animated cartoons called "Laugh-O-Grams." These were shown in a local neighborhood theater and were enthusiastically received. In a short time, Walt sold enough to buy his own camera and return the borrowed one to his boss.

Walt Disney decided to have the Faith to Pursue his Dream. Consequently, he struck out on his own and started the Laugh-O-Gram Company. Animated films such as "Little Red Riding Hood" and "Puss-n-Boots" gave the company a quick jump-start. Disney expanded the company by hiring additional staff.

However, his New York distributor did not send the percentages back to the Laugh-O-Gram Company. Walt Disney had to let everyone go. He even gave up his apartment and slept on pillows in the office. Soon he was broke and his company was finished.

The next couple of years were very bleak to say the least. He stated later that the only way he survived was because he liked eating beans. It was basically his only food. He traded cartoons for haircuts and occasionally received small amounts of cash by using his trade.

In 1923, he decided he would leave Kansas City and make a new start somewhere else. With $40 in his pocket, he boarded a train and moved to the West Coast. Hollywood was to be his new found "Promised Land." However, what he found in Hollywood brought further discouragement. Small studios were disappearing and job opportunities were scarce. The big giants, such as MGM, Universal, and Paramount, were not interested in the work of Walt Disney.

Finally, in desperation, Walt Disney borrowed $500 and started his own business with his brother Roy. He revived the old "Laugh-O-Gram" Company. Walt landed a contract with a New York distributor for a series of short subjects of "Alice in Cartoonland." Walt was offered $1500 a movie.

Profits soon were coming in and the future was looking bright. The Disney brothers were showing signs of a lucrative business. The hard work and never say die attitude was finally paying off. Everything they touched was turning to gold.

However, a strange development began to take place. The brother-in-law of the New York distributor was traveling to California each month to pick up the film. His popularity was growing with key employees of the Disneys'. Walt began to become suspicious of the man's motives.

Consequently, Walt Disney and his wife took a trip to New York. The purpose was to re-negotiate the contract. Walt was currently receiving $2250 per film and asked for a raise to $2500. However, the New York distributor offered Walt only $1800.

Walt Disney was told to take it or leave it. He also received a warning from the distributor who threatened to hire Walt's key employees away from him. The shocked and dismayed Disney turned down the offer. Sure enough, the distributor stole Disney's key employees, which nearly broke the back of Walt's company.

Walt Disney was thoroughly depressed and on the brink of despair. He went to the train station with his wife to begin the long trip home. His dream of owning his own company and providing for his family was crumbling before his very own eyes. His future seemed dark and gloomy. Walt had worked so hard and now it was gone. He and his wife boarded the train and Walt's heart was breaking in two.

However, the long coast to coast train ride was almost therapeutic. It seemed to be exactly what Walt needed. Soon his creative juices began to flow once again. His dream was being redefined not demolished. He began to get an idea for a new series of cartoons. Walt was sketching and drawing on the train with wild excitement. The train rambled on and his creativity grew with each mile. Walt Disney sat on the train and told his wife about the new series he would call "Mickey Mouse." The rest is history.

Yes, faith pursues your dream. Never forget, the darkest part of the night is just before the dawning of a new day. What if Walt Disney had thrown in the towel in discouragement on that train ride home? Why, his greatest achievement would have been buried through discouragement.

My friend, have faith in God and pursue your dream today. Let Jesus Christ live His life through you and you will do more than you could ever imagine. Ephesians 3:20-21 says:

Now to Him who is able to do exceedingly abundantly above all that we ask or think, according to the power that works in us, to Him be glory in the church by Christ Jesus to all generations, forever and ever. Amen

Yes, God will enable you to go beyond your wildest imagination as you glorify Christ through your life. Jesus died and rose again for your sins. He will give you a life of meaning and satisfaction. Put your faith in Christ and then pursue your God-given dream.

CHAPTER 24

TOMORROW'S DESTINY IS
THE RESULT OF TODAY'S DECISIONS

When Jacob, our youngest son, was only twelve years old, I had the opportunity to coach his little league All Star team. I was debating my decision when the thought hit me. "Twenty years from now do I want to look back and say -'I wish I had' or 'I'm glad I did?' " Therefore, I decided to coach the team. We experienced tremendous success as we won the district and finished state runner-up. Most importantly, we made lifelong friendships as coaches and taught life changing character to the boys.

This leads me to ask you, Do you find yourself saying, "I wish I had" or do you say "I'm glad I did"? In other words, do you live with regrets or are you satisfied with your life? People who live life to the fullest and achieve top-level performance understand that "tomorrow's destiny is the result of today's decisions." Give it all you have today because Psalm 118:24 says:

This is the day the Lord has made; We will rejoice and be glad in it.

It seems that many people are crucified between two thieves. The regrets of the past and the worries of the future. The sad reality is that both rob us of our energy and enthusiasm of today.

Let's face it; nobody can change what happened yesterday. After all, no one can turn back the hand of time and relive yesterday. Yet, far too many people drain valuable energy wishing they could change their past. They replay in their mind bad decisions, missed opportunities, and old memories of painful situations. However, the sad fact is that nothing in the past can be changed. We must let it go and move on.

Others look to future with fear. Many people spend precious time and energy worrying over things which they have absolutely no control. Think of all of the worry and fear that plagued many people over the year 2000. Many of the doomsdayers gave the impression that we would see worldwide chaos. Even many Christians acted like Jesus would step off His throne on January 1 of the year 2000.

Many people spent thousands of dollars preparing for the worst. Stockpiling food and supplies in fear that all would be lost. Some even purchased guns and ammunition to protect themselves during the potential worldwide disaster.

The point is this: We seldom make good use of our life regretting things of the past or worrying about the future. High-energy people and top achievers seize the moment of today. Yes, they will learn from the past in order to prepare for the future. However, they do not waste time and energy over situations they cannot change or cannot control.

The Apostle Paul certainly understood that "Tomorrow's destiny is the result of today's decisions." He did not spend valuable time regretting the past or worrying over the future. He focused on forgetting the past and reaching forward by faith. Listen to Philippians 3:13-14:

> *Brethren, I do not count myself to have apprehended; but one thing I do, forgetting those things which are behind and reaching forward to those things which are ahead. I press toward the goal for the prize of the upward call of God in Christ Jesus.*

Can you imagine the healing that would take place in homes if this were applied? Husbands and wives coming together at the cross and saying, "We will forget the things which are behind us and we will reach forward to those things which are ahead. We will look to the future with the peace of God reigning and ruling in our hearts."

Can you imagine the attitudes that would change when people stop regretting the past and worrying over the future? Think of the powerful impact we can have on each other with the simple positive attitude that says: "This is the day that the Lord has made, we will rejoice and be glad in it."

That's right my friend, God has given you today. Why not make the most of your God-given opportunity of today. Why not capitalize on your God-given potential beginning today. Simply choose to make a decision today that will shape your destiny tomorrow.

Do not look back on life and say, "I wish I had." Move away from the "Coulda, shoulda, woulda's." Make the kind of positive decisions that will cause you to say with great satisfaction: "I'm glad I did."

By the way, be sure and trust Christ as Savior today. The scripture says, "Today is the day of salvation." Yes, He offers us the free gift of eternal life through a personal relationship with Christ. All we need to do is invite Christ into our life by faith. Simply tell God that you believe Jesus died and rose again for your sins. Then by faith invite Christ into your life as Lord and Savior.

My friend, you make your decision for Christ and you will say from the bottom of your heart "I'm so glad I did."

Yes, "Tomorrows destiny is the result of today's decision." Do not live with regrets of the past or worries of the future. Let Jesus forgive the past and redirect your future. It is a path of true success that only Christ can give.

You know, several years ago I became the pastor of New Life Baptist Church. In the early years of ministry our children were very small. In fact, when we began serving the Lord in full time ministry our oldest child was only four and our youngest, at that time, was only two. Later on God blessed us with two more children.

However, from day one of becoming the pastor, I made up my mind that we would not neglect our family. I determined that our children would know their dad away from the pulpit. I determined in my heart that the ministry would not keep me from being an active father and spend time with the children.

Through the years I have had great joy in coaching their teams and simply being involved as a dad. It has been thrilling to watch the children grow. Eventually, I would hand the coaching baton on to others more qualified. However, the relationships developed through those events have been priceless. We always supported the children and cheered them on in the activities of their interest.

We have also always made family time a high priority. For years we would have a weekly "Family Night." This was precious time set aside to enjoy activities as a family. Many fond memories developed as a result of those "Family Nights."

An annual family vacation has also been a high priority. We have done many things, such as: renting a cabin, going camping, traveling west on a cross-country vacation, and going south to Florida and Disney World. We have also seen the Niagara Falls and, of course, gone to Cedar Point and ridden all the rides.

My point is the fact that we made a choice to keep our family a top priority. Cindi and I love each other and we love our four children. We have lived our lives without regrets.

Eventually, the day came for Cindi and I to take our oldest son, Michael, 800 miles away to college. It was a difficult time because we knew Michael would be greatly missed at home. He is a very positive role model for his two younger brothers and his younger sister has great admiration for him, as well. His influence on the family is very positive and his absence would be very painful. However, we were delighted with his decision to invest a year studying the Bible at the Word of Life Bible Institute in Scroon Lake, NY.

Finally, it came time to say good-bye. The lump in my throat was very large and the good bye was extremely difficult. Then we stood and watched our son jog off to his dorm. The years literally flashed before my eyes.

It seemed like yesterday when we shouted with joy at the birth of our firstborn. As he jogged away, I could see him taking his first steps as a baby. I could see him wearing his first soccer uniform. I could envision the little boy who got the game-winning hit in a little league game. I could see him in his wrestling singlet preparing for a big match. It all flashed before me as he trotted off to his dorm and went from a little boy to a young man right before my eyes.

I must admit that the emotion was nearly overwhelming. However, one thought struck me as I stood there. "I'm glad I was involved in his life." I'm glad I'm not standing here with regrets and saying, "I wish I had." I'm glad we raised him in the church. I'm glad he is interested in spiritual things. I'm glad we are positive role models for him. I'm glad we have many precious family memories. Even though I don't know what his future holds, I'm glad to know that I serve a God who does know.

My friend, live for Christ and you will be able to say, "I'm glad I did" and you will avoid saying, "I wish I had." Make proper decisions today to secure a positive destiny for tomorrow. Yes, "Tomorrow's destiny will be the result of today's decisions."

CHAPTER 25

HAPPINESS IS LEAVING THE WOODPILE A LITTLE HIGHER THAN YOU FOUND IT

The Scripture tells us, in Acts 20:35, that Jesus said, "It is more blessed to give than receive." This has been called the supreme beatitude because the word "blessed" means "Oh how very happy." In essence, Jesus is teaching the principle that true happiness is giving of yourself and your resources to make this world a better place to live. Happiness is leaving the woodpile a little higher than you found it.

Think of it this way. Suppose you lived in a day when wood was necessary for fuel. It was used to heat the house and cook the food. Firewood was a very important commodity.

Let's further suppose that people had a common woodpile to draw from. Anyone in the community was welcome to use the woodpile. It was simply understood that those who took from the woodpile should add to it, as well.

I believe you would find three kinds of people in that situation. Some would put back exactly the amount they used. They would contribute to the community woodpile no more or no less than they used.

Others would put back less than they used. After all, it is work to cut wood for the community. Someone else would have to make it up. They would figure that plenty of people would give more and pick up the slack.

However, a third group would add more to the pile than what they took from it. They would go above and beyond the call of duty. They would want to be a blessing to others and not a burden to the community. For them, happiness is leaving the woodpile a little higher than they found it.

Can you imagine what life would be like if this was applied to the family, the workplace, and the community. The atmosphere in the home and on the job and in the community would change overnight. People would go from living selfishly to living selflessly.

Many of our everyday problems would be solved. Common struggles would disappear as people would once again; go the extra mile for others. Tension in the home would disappear. Power struggles on the job would vanish away. Community standards would rise as people looked out for one another.

Jesus said in Luke 6:38:

Give, and it will be given to you: good measure, pressed down, shaken together, and running over will be put in your bosom. For with the same measure that you use, it will be measured back to you.

We could say that life is like an echo, what you give out is what you get back. Yes, giving to others will bring a blessing to you. I believe that unselfish giving is a real key to joyful living. True happiness is found in helping others. Giving to meet the needs of others helps us get our eyes off of our own problems. Some of the most miserable people are those with a selfish outlook on life.

However, the truly happy and well-adjusted person is the generous soul. Selfish living is the result of immaturity. After all, the first word that most babies learn is "mine." That old trio of "me, myself, and I" can truly be a selfish and unhappy world. Mature people, on the other hand, experience the joy of living on a higher plane.

Let me share with you some things that you can give that will not cost you a dime. However, the rich reward it will bring to others is priceless.

To begin with, you can give a smile. This will be a tremendous blessing to others. In fact, people will often smile back in return. If you are looking at sad and grouchy faces all day, you may want to look in the mirror and see what your face is saying. Smile and the world will smile back at you.

Proverbs 17:22 says,

A merry heart does good like medicine.

Yes, there is actually medicinal value in smiling. By the way, it takes less work to smile, as well. They say that more muscles are involved in making a frown than in smiling. Believe me, frowning is not worth the extra work. Give someone a gift of health through a cheerful smile today.

Next, how about giving someone a pat on the back. You know, it is a short distance between a pat on the back and a kick in the pants, but it makes all the difference in the world. People need the positive affirmation that a "pat on the back" can bring.

Give someone a sincere compliment. Perhaps affirm a character quality that you admire. Reinforce qualities like faithfulness, honesty, integrity, loyalty, and hard work. Remember, talent is what someone has, while character is something you are. Recognize and compliment a character quality.

Give someone a word of encouragement. Build up someone today. To encourage is to inspire someone with hope and courage. Proverbs 12:25 says:

Anxiety in the heart of man causes depression, but a good word makes it glad.

Here's something you can give that will be a blessing to others. Give someone the "benefit of the doubt." This will strengthen your relationship with others. You will build on the foundation of loyalty and trust which is a winning combination.

How about giving someone a "listening ear"? You know, the good Lord gave us one mouth and two ears. Using them accordingly could be very wise. Dale Carnegie, author of the book, *How to Win Friends and Influence People* said, "You can make more friends in two months by becoming interested in other people than you can in two years by trying to get other people interested in you." Listening to someone lets them know you care about them. It also communicates, to them, their value in your eyes.

Other things you could give include:

1. Give an old friend a call; perhaps you need to mend a broken fence. Make the final move. You'll be glad you did.

2. You could give a helping hand to a worthy cause. We all feel better when we volunteer our efforts for something worthwhile. Donate some time to your church or a community project. You'll feel good about yourself as you give something back to your community.

3. How about giving a child a gift of your time. It will be an investment worth making.

4. Give someone your prayers. After all, we could all use a little "help from above."

Another thing you can give someone is a positive attitude. Make sure your attitude is worth catching. Basically, we are talking about giving your love to others. Doing simple acts of kindness to brighten someone's world.

You know, Jesus certainly left the woodpile a little higher than He found it. He created the trees to be cut for the woodpile. Then He took from the woodpile enough lumber to construct the old rugged cross. Then Jesus died on the cross and paid the penalty for the sins of the world. The Bible says it was for the "joy that was set before Him that He endured the cross."

My friend, the joy that Jesus experienced at the cross of Calvary was the gift He was offering to humanity. Jesus died and rose again for our sins so we could experience a relationship with God. The Bible says there is joy in heaven when one person comes to know Christ as Savior.

Once we trust in Christ, we have the power to live selflessly instead of selfishly. It has been said that selfishness turns life into burdens. However, selflessness turns burdens into life. Yes my friend, happiness is leaving the woodpile a little higher than you found it.

CHAPTER 26

TEAM IS DEFINED AS:
TOGETHER EVERYONE ACCOMPLISHES MORE

People working together can always accomplish greater things than an individual working alone. It has been said "there is no letter I in the word TEAM." Consequently, the word TEAM has been properly defined as: Together Everyone Accomplishes More.

The late and great coach Vince Lombardi said the following concerning teamwork. He said that "individual commitment to a group effort - that is what makes a team work, a company work, a society work, a civilization work." He also said, "Teamwork is what the Green Bay Packers were all about. They didn't do it for individual glory, they did it because they love one another." Lombardi went on to say, "The love I speak of is loyalty, the love I speak of is teamwork, the love one man has for another."

Yes, make no mistake about it. Teamwork is crucial in athletics and vitally important in the game of life. Here's something to consider - Teamwork is so important that God Himself said in Genesis 2:18:

It is not good that man should be alone; I will make Him a helper comparable to him.

When you think about it, God created the family unit as the first team structure to help us in the game of life.

Yes, God certainly intends for people to work together. God also instructs us in His Word to learn the value of teamwork in order to encourage others and help one another along in the journey of life.

Consider Ecclesiastes 4:9-10 and verse 12.

Two are better than one, because they have a good reward

for their labor. For if they fall, one will lift up his compan-ion. But woe to him who is alone when he falls, for he has no one to help him. Though one may be overpowered by another, two can withstand him. And a threefold cord is not quickly broken.

Essentially, God is saying that we need each other. Life has its share of "bumps in the road" and occasional "setbacks." However, people who travel the road of life together and work together will have an advantage over the one who determines to go alone. Basically, God is teaching the concept that together everyone accomplishes more.

I saw this principle unfold one season as I cheered for my son, Joseph, and the Mishawaka Varsity Wrestling Team. It seems like he was born for the sport of wrestling with his aggressive nature and fierce competitive spirit. It was always exciting to watch Joseph and his teammates conquer their opponents. Their success during the 1999-2000 season all boiled down to one word: TEAM. The incredible accomplishment of State Runner-up was the dedi-cated and collective efforts of the entire team.

I am convinced their journey to the state finals began all the way back on the first day of practice. The coaching staff taught the vital importance of teamwork. Teaching the value of the TEAM is not an easy task in an individual sport like wrestling. However, they did a tremendous job of building a team spirit.

The coach did more than prepare the wrestlers to compete as individuals. He molded the athletes into a team. In fact, they became like a family. They truly cared about each other and the col-lective success of the team.

The family spirit was the number one trademark of the team. They learned to encourage one another by observing the way the coaches encouraged the team. Win or lose, the coaches always respected the dignity of the wrestler and constantly built them up with encouragement.

Therefore, the family spirit was developed with positive reinforcement. After all, loving families stick together and support one another through "thick or thin." Tight knit families applaud a victory of a family member and encourage the one who has experienced disappointment. Loving family members do not kick each other when they are down. They simply pick each other up and help them onto their feet again.

Well, as you can imagine, the team pulled together like a close-knit family and experienced tremendous success. The important thing was that every wrestler made a significant contribution at some point for the team during the state tourney. Sometimes it was found in a wrestler who defeated an opponent in the tourney that he had lost to in the regular season. Sometimes it was gaining a few extra points for the team by pinning their opponent. Sometimes it was an "unsung hero" pulling out a fierce battle for the team.

Sometimes it was competing with the heart of a lion and fighting to the finish to give up as few team points as possible in a defeat. Every time, the goal was always the same, dig deep down and give the extra effort for the team. Bottom line, it was not a group of individuals simply doing their own thing as they tallied a team score. Oh no, it ran much deeper than that. It was a team working together for a common goal.

They advanced through the tournament and made it to the state finals. With only eight teams remaining, fierce competition was in store as the best of the best from the state of Indiana squared off against each other. It was a showdown taken right out of the pages of the "Old West." The crowd had gathered and the streets had been cleared for an old fashioned "gunfight at the OK Corral."

Just two days before the showdown, the Cavemen were given the news that a wrestler in the starting lineup had become ineligible. However, the Cavemen refused to flinch and faced the adversity as a team. They demonstrated the type of determination that is only found in the hearts of champions.

They began by defeating sixth ranked and state powerhouse, Belmont. It was an intense war that came right down to the wire. Mishawaka brought the fans to their feet with a thunderous roar as they won the highly emotional battle in the closest meet in the history of the state tourney.

Next came the second ranked team from Franklin, who had previously defeated Mishawaka for their only loss of the season. Now it was time for a rematch. The wresters dug deep down and found the incredible strength from the well of their soul. Every team member gave it all they had as they won another fierce battle.

Mishawaka had been victorious in back to back meets that were the closest scores in the history of the state tourney. It was the type of accomplishment that can only be achieved with an incredible team spirit that pulled together like one big family.

Yes, the Cavemen finally bowed out to Evansville's Mater-Dei, as Mishawaka finished state runner-up. However, the important thing was that a group of young men clearly demonstrated the "TEAM concept"—together everyone accomplishes more.

By the way, Almighty God invites us to join His team. God sent His Son, the Lord Jesus Christ, to die on the cross for our sins. He paid in full our sin debt to God. He rose again the third day and offers the free gift of eternal life to all who believe in Him.

Yes, 2000 years ago, Jesus Christ scored the greatest victory for the entire human race team. It was no contest when Jesus scored a take down on Satan and immediately pinned him at the cross. God the Father blew the whistle and slapped the mat, as the nails were driven into the hands and feet of His Son. At that moment, the enemy was soundly defeated without the opportunity to even score a single point.

My friend, Jesus did not allow any reversals and He certainly did not permit Satan to escape. This triumphant victory brought the angels of heaven to their feet and the applause rang out for the entire world to hear.

Jesus demonstrated His love for the entire human race when He sacrificed His life on the cross for our sins. John 3:16 says:

For God so loved the world that He gave His only begotten Son, that whoever believes in Him should not perish, but have everlasting life.

Yes, God loves the entire world and invites us to join His team by faith in His Son. Joining His team means you will not only experience the peace and pardon of forgiveness, you will also have the Lord as your friend and His Word will be your guide.

As your friend, the Lord will always be there to pick you up when you are down. As your guide, His Word will always direct you in the right path. My friend, team up with the Lord and you will discover that together, with the Lord, everyone accomplishes more.

CHAPTER 27

BLESSED IS THE NATION WHOSE GOD IS THE LORD

I believe the United States of America is the greatest nation in the world! I am proud to say that I am a flag waving, patriotic American. I am grateful for the freedom we experience in our great land of opportunity. I am also grateful to God for our rich spiritual heritage. Psalm 33:12 says:

Blessed is the nation whose God is the Lord.

Yes, I am convinced that our founding fathers established our country upon Biblical principles. For example, in April of 1607, when the first settlers founded the Jamestown Colony at Cape Henry, they erected a large wooden cross and held a public prayer meeting. On November 11, 1611, when the Mayflower Pact was signed at Cape Cod, they stated that their purpose was for the "glory of God and the advancement of the Christian faith." Then on December 16, 1611, when they reached the Plymouth Harbor, they "fell on their knees and blessed the God of heaven."

My friend, these were Christian people with high moral standards who bravely sailed to America in search of religious freedom. Their goal was to establish families, communities, and schools, which honored Almighty God. Churches were built by the Puritans before they would build their own houses. The entire community attended church to listen to the pastor as he preached the Word of God. It was the Biblical teaching in the house of worship that shaped our nation.

Patrick Henry, who said, "give me liberty or give me death", also said this. "I would only wish that I could leave my family my faith in Jesus Christ, for without that, nothing else is worthwhile." Benjamin Franklin said, "God surely was no idle spectator when this great nation was born in His name and with His grace." In 1787, when they were struggling to write the constitution, Benjamin Franklin quoted Psalm 127:1,

Unless the Lord builds the house, they labor in vain who build it.

Then he called for two days of prayer.

Our Declaration of Independence says, "All men are created equal and are endowed by their creator with certain unalienable rights, that among these are life, liberty, and the pursuit of happiness." These were men who believed in God. Our founding fathers held strong convictions in the ethical teachings of the Bible. Someone once pointed to a Bible on Andrew Jackson's desk and asked why it was there. He pointed to the Bible and said, "that Book, sir, is the rock on which our republic rests."

Yes, make no mistake about it, God has blessed this nation because our forefathers sought to honor the Almighty. Even our coins say, "In God We Trust." I thank God for our spiritual heritage and the blessing of God upon America.

I also thank God for those who protect our freedom. We have the greatest military in the world. Our political democracy is strong and our military defense is superior to all other nations. Our brave men and women in the armed forces are committed to sacrificial service for our country. They are even willing to give the ultimate sacrifice of their own life in order to protect our way of living. As one nation under God, we have the secure hand of God to guide us and the military strength to protect us.

I also thank God for our police officers and fire fighters. These brave people serve our great nation with great sacrifice. They daily put their life on the line to keep our lives safe and secure. Our country was reminded of the brave sacrifice of these men and women during the terrorist attack on America. These dedicated and selfless people were a shining example of the indestructible American spirit.

Yes, September 11, 2001, is a day that we will never forget. The terrorist attack on America was a tragedy that shook our nation to the core. It was a devastating event that took the lives of many innocent people. We will always pray for the families of the victims as they seek to somehow rebuild their lives. We pray that God will sustain them with His love.

However, one thing became very apparent in the midst of this tragedy. While the terrorists were able to bring destruction upon humanity, they were unable to destroy the faith of humanity. The American spirit is strong and our faith is alive and well! Once again, we demonstrated a humble faith in Almighty God as people gathered around the nation and sought His help through prayer. Yes, God will bless America because "Blessed is the nation whose God is the Lord."

You know, shortly after the Revolutionary War, the French political philosopher, Alexis de Tocquerville, came to the United States. He came searching for the magic quality that enabled so few colonists to defeat the vast British army. He visited the harbors, our fertile fields, and our vast natural resources. He visited our schools and also read our constitution. He still could not find this magic quality that inspired such courage in the people.

Then he visited our churches. He found the pulpits on fire for God. It was at that time he found the secret to our strength. He returned to France and wrote these words, "America is great because America is good. And if America ceases to be good, America will cease to be great!"

My friend, I believe a grass roots movement of "goodness" is at work in our nation today. People from all walks of life are joining together in the true patriotic spirit. People of faith are united in prayer to Almighty God and asking for His strength to sustain us in our hour of need. Many people are putting "shoe leather" to their prayers as they extend the hand of mercy in volunteer service for humanity.

Yes, a spiritual awakening is sweeping our land. Let us look to the Almighty God and submit ourselves to the teachings of His Word. Rest assured, as we follow the Lord and build on His truth, God will continue to bless America. After all, "Blessed is the nation whose God is the Lord."

CHAPTER 28

PEOPLE INFLUENCE PEOPLE

It is amazing how modern technology has changed our culture. People can virtually live an isolated life if they so choose. After all, we have online banking and shopping, ATMs, stores with automatic checkouts, gas payments at the pumps, fax machines, etc. All of these things make it possible to develop a lifestyle that totally removes us from personal contact with people. However, never forget: "People influence people."

Let's face it; all of us have been shaped one way or another by various people. Most of us can think back to some special people who have influenced us in a positive way. The Scripture affirms this principle in Proverbs 27:17 which says:

As iron sharpens iron, So a man sharpens the countenance of his friend.

Yes, the Word of God is clear: People can have a positive influence on people. In fact, the people who surround you are much more important than the problems you face. A positive person will sharpen your countenance and lift your spirit. For example, the Scripture says in I Samuel 23:16 that Jonathan went to David and "strengthened his hand in God." Yes, Jonathan was a faithful friend who inspired David to become a great leader.

Moses influenced Joshua and developed him into a great leader, as well. Deuteronomy 31:7-8 describes how Moses affirmed Joshua in the presence of the people as he passed the leadership baton on to him. He challenged Joshua to "be strong and of good courage" and encouraged him with the promise that "the Lord would be with him."

In the New Testament, we discover that Andrew influenced Peter to follow Christ. The Bible tells in John 1:41-42 that Andrew believed in Jesus and introduced his brother Peter to Christ as well. The rest is history. Peter became a great leader of the early church because his brother cared enough to bring him to Jesus. We could go on and on. Bottom line, "people influence people."

When I think back on my life growing up, many positive people had an influence on me at an early age. One particular person was my first little league coach. His name was Don Shepherd and he was in his early twenties. His younger brother, Willie, was only eight years old and Don was like a father figure to him. Therefore, he decided to tackle the job of coaching eight and nine-year-old boys in little league.

He was a great coach! I loved playing baseball for Don Shepherd. He never yelled at us. He patiently taught a group of eager minds the game of baseball. Don was a great encourager. I always wanted to give everything I had and do my very best for him. Don's coaching made my first little league experience a very positive memory.

Don had taught Willie how to pitch and we needed a catcher. For an eight-year-old boy, Willie had a blazing fastball. Most of the kids did not want to even try to catch for Willie. I remember Don asking me if I wanted to give it a try. I was more than ready to get behind the plate. Therefore, Don patiently worked with me and instructed me on how to be an effective catcher.

First, I had to learn not to blink my eyes when the batter would swing the bat. Don taught me to always keep my eye on the ball. He showed me how to block a pitch that went into the dirt. It was an exciting position and I loved being in on the action. Willie would often strike out the side and Don would make me feel like a million dollars. Everyone loved playing for Don.

After the game, we would all head to the root beer stand. We always had a lot of fun! Yes, we won the league that year. However, what I remember most was the positive influence of my first little league coach. He cared about the kids and he made it a positive experience for a group of young boys.

You know, I believe that much of my success as a volunteer coach is the result of my positive experience with my very first coach. I have learned the value of encouragement and positive affirmation. It is exciting to instill confidence in young athletes and watch their self-esteem develop as they learn to achieve success.

I remember a group of ten-year-old boys that I coached one year on an all-star team. They were trailing by eight runs going into their final at bat. We called the boys into the dugout and told them to believe in themselves. We encouraged them to simply take it one step at a time by getting one hit at a time. The end result was a miracle finish as the boys scored nine runs in the final inning to win the regional. Most importantly, it was an opportunity to teach the team that any obstacle could be overcome when you work together. The life lesson was far more valuable than the victory.

I have had the privilege of seeing some of the young athletes that I have coached through the years mature into outstanding community leaders. For example, one summer we took a group of teenagers to the inner city of Chicago for volunteer work. Three of the key leaders were young men who I had coached in elementary football a few years prior. They volunteered their time and energy to help demonstrate the love of God to some inner city kids who desperately hungered for spiritual encouragement.

Yes, people influence people. My friend, volunteer some time and make a positive investment in the lives of others. God will use your influence to impact the community as you teach positive values and life skills. Never forget, Proverbs 27:17 says: "As iron sharpens iron, So a man sharpens the countenance of his friend."

Yes, sharpen someone's life and God will use you in a positive way. Remember, in the midst of our high tech culture there are still some things that require the personal touch. After all, God uses people to influence people.

CHAPTER 29

ROUGH WEATHER BUILDS STRONG TIMBER

Perhaps you or someone you love has been going through a tough time. It seems as if the storms of life are blowing right into your face. The waves of adversity may be violently and relentlessly beating upon your life. You may feel like you are up to your neck in problems, which beg for solutions. Well remember this: Rough weather builds strong timber.

God is grooming you for something special. In fact, Psalm 119:71 says:

It is good for me that I have been afflicted, that I may learn Your statutes.

The Scripture goes on to say in Psalm 119:92:

Unless Your law had been my delight, I would then have perished in my affliction.

Perhaps you are familiar with the story of a tour group, which visited a furniture manufacturing plant. This particular manufacturer was well known for producing the highest quality furniture. Some of the finest furnishings were hand crafted and the tour group was privileged to observe the craftsmanship. Their skillful work of art was a beauty to behold.

The tour also included a visit to the wood mill located next door. It was a wonderful opportunity to observe the process of selecting the wood to be used for such outstanding quality furniture. The worker would carefully inspect each piece as he sorted through a large pallet of wood. He separated the wood into one of two distinct piles.

The first pile was a large stack of wood. This particular pile of wood was marked "discard." To the naked eye it appeared fine, but the trained observer quickly separated the wood for common use.

The other pile was much smaller in size. The wood was marked "good." This meant it was of high enough quality to be used to manufacture their finest furniture. Only this particular wood was allowed for the choicest craftsmanship.

One of the onlookers from the tour was a little puzzled at the selections. He asked the worker why the wood was being separated in such a manner. After all, the wood looked the same to the untrained observer of the tour group. It seemed like such a waste to get rid of so much wood. It also seemed like it would take forever to come up with enough wood to make a piece of furniture.

The worker explained the criteria for separating the wood between common use and high quality production. The wood, which was separated for common use, had come from trees in the valley. Those trees had been protected from the storms through the years. As a result, the grain of wood was rather coarse. It was only good for common lumber.

However, the wood marked "good" came from the trees that grew high on the mountains. Because the trees had come from the mountaintops, they had not been protected from the rough weather. Therefore, from the time the trees were very small, they had been beaten by the strong winds. These trees had grown up facing extreme adversity, such as violent rainstorms and the harshness of direct sunlight beating down upon them.

Consequently, the trees had been toughened through the years. Along with strengthening the trees, the storms also gave the lumber a fine grain. Therefore, those pieces of wood were used for the finest furniture. The worker explained that the choice wood is too good to be used for ordinary lumber. It was reserved for their highest grade and greatest quality of craftsmanship.

You see my friend; rough weather builds strong timber. The same is true in life. People who have weathered the storms of life have gained a wealth of wisdom to share. They are always the finest of people and often used by God for His most delicate work.

Let's go back to Psalm 119:71 where the Scripture says:

It is good for me that I have been afflicted, that I may learn Your statutes.

In other words, the psalmist learned the value of the Word of God during times of trouble. The struggles of life shaped his values in life. Psalm 119:72 says:

The law of Your mouth is better to me than thousands of coins of gold and silver.

The psalmist claims the Word of God became more precious to him than money. You see, money can buy temporary happiness, but it cannot buy you permanent joy. Money can buy you a house, but it cannot make it a peaceful home. Money can help you make a living, but it cannot teach you how to live or give you peace of mind. Anchoring your faith in Jesus and trusting completely in His Word is the only way to have inner peace that surpasses all human understanding. Yes, your faith will even help you discover the positive aspects of life's challenges. James 1:2-3 says:

My brethren, count it all joy when you fall into various trials, knowing that the testing of your faith produces patience.

You see, God allows us to face various struggles in order to strengthen our faith and teach us the faithfulness of God. Other people are also drawn to Christ as they observe your faith during challenging times. People recognize the importance of eternal values during earthly problems. As a result, God becomes very real to you as you discover His Word as your power source for living.

My friend, even Jesus went through rough weather as He was stretched out on the strong timber of the cross. He died and rose again as a demonstration of God's love for you. Consequently, God wants to mold your life into a beautiful work of craftsmanship for His glory. Therefore, He will use the storms of life to shape you into one of God's finest handiworks of His grace. Yes, rough weather builds strong timber.

136

CHAPTER 30

TALENT MAY GET YOU TO THE TOP, BUT IT TAKES CHARACTER TO KEEP YOU THERE

Developing a life of character will protect the "rising star" of today from becoming the "falling star" of tomorrow. Yes, it takes time to develop the type of championship character that is required to build a successful life. Ultimately, our success or failure will be measured over the long haul of life. After all, "Talent may get you to the top, but it takes character to keep you there."

Even our journey of faith is often described as a "walk with God." For example, the Scripture tells us in Micah 6:8 to "walk humbly with your God." Colossians 1:10 states, "have a walk worthy of the Lord, fully pleasing Him." In II Corinthians 5:7, we are encouraged to "walk by faith." Yes, our spiritual journey is a marathon not a hundred-yard dash.

I'm reminded of two young pitchers who were just getting started in professional baseball a number of years ago. The year was 1968 and one young man was in the very early stages of his career and the other was in his rookie season. Two young men with comparable talent, but the contrast of their careers became as different as night and day.

The first young man was Denny McClain, who in 1968 won 31 games for the Detroit Tigers. He was considered a young pitching sensation. He accomplished what very few have ever done in professional baseball. Winning 31games in one season was phenomenal. He also won the cherished Cy Young award and had a very promising future.

He received all kinds of national attention as sportswriters dominated their articles with the young pitching sensation from Detroit.

Little League ballplayers all wanted to wear his number. Old men sat on their front porches and talked about the talented young man who was "skyrocketing into stardom." He was literally the talk of baseball and was well on his way to becoming a superstar.

Unfortunately, he "fell from grace" a couple of years later. He was busted on a gambling charge and suspended from baseball. He became nothing more than a mere "flash in the pan." Today he is a distant memory because he lacked the character to go the distance.

In 1968, Nolan Ryan was a rookie for the New York Mets. His record was a mere six wins and nine losses. The same year the "young pitching sensation from Detroit" won 31 games, the "rookie from New York" only won six games. The press did not give Nolan Ryan any attention, but this did not stop him from his goal to succeed. He decided to outwork everyone else during the off-season. In fact, his work ethic became the ultimate trademark of his lifelong success.

He went on to pitch many, many years in professional baseball. Nolan Ryan won over 320 games and had over 5000 career strikeouts. He also pitched seven no hitters during his professional career. Many believe that his career strike out record may be untouchable. Eventually, *Sports Illustrated* called Nolan Ryan a "Living Legend" and a "Modern Day Miracle."

The difference between the two athletes was not found in their talent. The difference was in their character. Nolan Ryan had a championship career because he lived a life marked with championship character. Yes, "Talent may get you to the top but it takes character to keep you there."

My friend, the Bible gives a blueprint for developing Championship Character. Colossians 3:23-24 says:

> *And whatever you do, do it heartily, as to the Lord and not to men, knowing that from the Lord you will receive the reward of the inheritance; for you serve the Lord Christ.*

The Apostle Paul gives a blueprint to develop championship character. He says, in essence, championship character begins with commitment. The Scripture says, "do it heartily." In other words, put your heart and soul into your efforts. It has been said that nothing great ever happens on the OK level.

Paul is saying that champions rise above the OK level. The word "heartily" means to do it with enthusiasm. The late Harry Truman said, "Every great achievement is the story of a flaming heart." My friend, when God is at work in you then your heart will be on fire for Him. This will produce a commitment to His cause. Championship character begins with the commitment of giving 110% to all you do.

Next, championship character includes conviction. God tells us to do it heartily "as to the Lord." This gives us the concept of conviction, which is our belief system. My friend, what are the beliefs that affect the very core of your being? What are the foundational values that you build your life on?

This draws us to the importance of developing your convictions from a reliable source of authority. I suggest that you find your values from the Word of God. You cannot go wrong building your life on the truth of Scripture. After all, the Bible is not a rulebook to make you miserable; it is a roadmap to make you successful.

Finally, we also discover that championship character includes confidence. God promises to reward us as we serve the Lord. My friend, here is the good news; God keeps His promises. You can rest assured that Jesus will reward your life as you live for Him.

You know, I have the privilege of serving as the volunteer chaplain for the Varsity Football Team at Mishawaka High School. Each week during the season, we have a fifteen-minute inspirational and motivational "chapel service." The players come on a volunteer basis and we meet in the locker room before school on the day of the game. My goal is to help develop character in young people of today who will help lead the community of tomorrow. We often emphasize the concept that talent may get you to the top, but it takes character to keep you there. Consequently, we instruct the players on principles of faith that develop character in life. Our strategy is to help improve their life skills as we relate the game of football to life.

My friend, follow Jesus and you will develop the character of a champion. You will have the credibility for the long haul of life. Talent alone may quickly fade away like the brief career of a young pitching sensation. However, championship character can produce lasting success in life like the legendary example of the hardworking Nolan Ryan. Yes, Talent may get you to the top but it takes character to keep you there.

CHAPTER 31

INTEGRITY IS THE
INFLUENCE OF A GENUINE LIFE

Proverbs 22:1 says:

A good name is to be chosen rather than great riches,
Loving favor rather than silver and gold.

Yes, integrity builds a "good name." You will lead a life of respectability that upholds your name. You will leave your children something to live up to by "keeping your name honorable" in the community.

Integrity essentially means "What you see is what you get." The dictionary defines integrity as: uprightness, soundness of character, moral wholeness. You could say that integrity is the "first cousin" of honesty. In many ways they are very similar. Honesty deals with the truthfulness of the words that we say, while integrity deals with the truthfulness of the life that we lead. Therefore, it could be said that Integrity is the Influence of a Genuine Life.

I will never forget the greatest lesson I learned about integrity. It happened one summer day in high school as I worked for my father. My dad was a self-employed bricklayer with his own crew. My three brothers and myself learned the work ethic by mixing mortar and carrying bricks each summer.

However, on this particular day, I learned more than just the work ethic. I learned a powerful lesson on integrity. My dad had just hired a new bricklayer and he was working on the back wall of the house. We worked hard all morning and then took a break for lunch. That is when the lesson on integrity began.

Dad went back and examined the new man's work. It was obvious to the "trained eye" that the new man's work did not measure up to the standard of my father. Without hesitation, my dad began removing the bricks from the wall. One by one the mortar was scraped off the bricks and the entire wall would be redone. The new bricklayer stood by my father's side as dad showed him the standard of excellence that was expected.

Dad had a high standard of quality that would not be compromised. Dad worked as if his name went on every job. Therefore, it was more important to my dad to sacrifice short-term profit to maintain a lifetime of integrity. Many people would have overlooked the sub-standard work. After all, it was on the back of the house. Who would even notice? Well, my dad noticed and his integrity made sure the home was bricked correctly.

You see, there are some things that money cannot buy. Integrity is one of them. I learned that lesson one hot summer afternoon by observing my father. It was certainly a day when I learned the true "bricks and mortar" of a life of character. Yes, integrity is the influence of a genuine life.

A person of integrity has nothing to hide. Your public life does not fear a private examination. Integrity will shine brightly in the midst of intense scrutiny. D.L. Moody said that: "Your character is what a person is in the dark." In other words, your true character is who you are when nobody is watching you.

I believe that integrity is the cornerstone of the foundation of your life. Integrity will be more committed to ethical principles than economic profits. Integrity will be committed to the long-term effects instead of short-term results. Integrity will never be sacrificed on the altar of the immediate. A person of integrity will not short cut their character in order to achieve a goal. After all, true success has no shortcuts.

Jesus described two builders in the conclusion of His Sermon on the Mount. He described a wise builder and a foolish builder. One building had a proper foundation, while the other was built on the sand. One house was the true substance, while the other was a mere image. One stood the test of time, while the other fell in time. One demonstrated grace under pressure, while the other collapsed under pressure.

Jesus said in Matthew 7:24-25:

Therefore whoever hears these saying of Mine, and does them, I will liken him to a wise man who built his house on the rock: and the rain descended, the floods came, and the winds blew and beat on that house; and it did not fall, for it was founded on the rock.

Yes, the Master Teacher had profound things to say about building with integrity. Jesus was not meeting with the local "home builders association." They were not preparing for the annual "Panorama of Homes." Jesus was instructing people on building a life of integrity. Jesus was teaching that a genuine life of integrity will withstand the storms of adversity. It has been said that character is not created in a crisis, it is simply revealed.

My friend, the scripture says, "Faith without works is dead." Yes, the true believer will not only learn God's Word, but will also live God's Word. Jesus said that a person who listens to Him and follows His teaching will be a wise person. Obedience to Christ is building your life on the "Rock Solid Foundation." It leads to blessing not bondage.

In fact, obedience to Christ will give you confidence in His Word. You will quickly discover that His Word is true. You will learn that His Word is the way of wisdom. You will experience the joy of living under the Lordship of Christ. Your heart will rejoice as you experience the blessing of God.

This will enable you to keep building on the proper foundation. You will be ready to take the next step of faith. Each step along the way will increase your foundation of faith. The gradual progress will increase your faith in God's power. The end result will be a life of integrity. This will give you the positive influence and a powerful impact in the lives of others.

You see my friend, a life of integrity means you can be trusted. One of the important lessons of life is the fact that a person must be able to be trusted in everything. In fact, one of the sad realities of life is that you must be able to trust someone on all points or you cannot trust the person on any point. That is why integrity in leadership is extremely important. You cannot separate a leader's private life from his or her public perception. In fact, if the public perception is not real then you merely have "public deception." A leader must have integrity in order to have a genuine influence. It has been said that:

Many succeed momentarily by what they know,

Some succeed temporarily by what they do; but

few succeed permanently by what they are.

Perhaps you remember the Tylenol crisis that took place some years ago. Several people were poisoned to death. The investigators traced the cause of the deaths to contaminated Tylenol capsules. It became a moment of truth for the company. How would they handle the problem?

The president of the company ordered all Tylenol capsules to be removed from the store shelves. The decision to pull the capsules was made in less than an hour and cost the company over 100 million dollars. A reporter asked the president of the company how he could make such an expensive decision so quickly. The president explained that he was simply practicing the company's mission statement that said they would "operate with honesty and integrity."

My friend, when you know what you stand for, it is easy to make the right decision. Whether it is a president of a large corporation tackling a national crisis or a self-employed bricklayer who is simply putting his name on his work, the principle of Proverbs 22:1 is the same. "A good name is to be chosen rather than great riches."

Yes, integrity is the influence of a genuine life.

CHAPTER 32

RESPECT IS LIKE A BOOMERANG—WHAT YOU SEND OUT IS WHAT WILL OFTEN BE RETURNED

I believe there are some basic character qualities that help us become champions in the game of life. Your reputation is what others think you are, but your character is what you truly are. Your reputation could be simply an image, but your character is the true substance. In terms of character, respect must be an important quality. I fully believe that respect is like a boomerang-what you send out is what will often be returned

Jesus said in Matthew 7:12:

However you want people to treat you, so treat them.

We call it the golden rule. "Do unto others as you want them to do unto you." Yes, we are to treat people with the same type of dignity and respect that we would desire for ourselves.

My friend, this principle is the very heart and soul of all human relationships. It is important to live your life on the foundational principle of mutual respect. In fact, Jesus said that the entire demonstration of our faith hinges on this principle of respect. You could say that the outworking of our faith is revealed in our respect for others.

Calvin Murphy, a former NFL running back, said this about respect: "I judge a person's worth by the kind of person he is in life; by the way he treats his fellow man, by the way he wants to be treated and by the way he respects people around him." Yes, make no mistake about it; people will judge our faith by the respect we show for others. I fully believe that "respect is like a boomerang-what you send out is what you will usually receive back."

I also believe that true respect must be earned not demanded.

When you demand the respect of others you will often times build an attitude of resentment. However, when you earn the respect of others, you will be rewarded with their loyalty.

For example, the husband that is harsh and demanding in the home will build resentment from his wife and children. There will be a tension in the home. Eventually the resentment may turn into a spirit of rebellion. The foolish husband may become angry and even more demanding. The sad reality will be a home on a collision course headed straight for the divorce court.

However, the husband who follows the scriptural teaching of servant leadership will experience peace and harmony. Ephesians 5:25 says: "Husbands, love your wives, just as Christ also loved the church and gave Himself for her." Yes, leadership by example will earn the respect of your family. A spirit of love and harmony will permeate the home. Resentment will be replaced with genuine respect. The boomerang principle of mutual respect can be related to any relationship.

Let's also consider why we should respect all people. The Bible says in Genesis 1:27:

So God created man in His own image; in the image of God
He created him; male and female He created them.

To be created in the image of God means you have the capacity to have fellowship with Him. Every human being has a mind to think, emotions to feel; and a will to choose. God allows you the freedom to choose a relationship with God through faith in Christ. God has placed a divine spark in each individual with the capacity of lighting the torch of faith. Therefore, every human being has incredible value and tremendous potential.

Since all people have been created in God's image; then respect for all people should be demonstrated. You may not approve of all behavior, but we are to show respect for the person. In fact, our love for God will be revealed in our repect for others.

Christ stated in Luke 10:27:

You shall love the Lord your God with all your heart, with all your soul, and with all your strength, and with all your mind, and your neighbor as yourself.

We call this the great commandment. Love for God and respect for humanity.

Motivational speaker, Zig Ziglar, tells the story of a woman who attended one of his seminars. She was completely sick of her job and decided to see if she could get motivated for a new career. She was completely "fed up" and ready to quit. She felt like no one respected her and she was ready to "throw in the towel."However, after attending the motivational seminar she decided to make a personal change. It seems that Zig Zigler challenged her to change her actions and see if her attitude would change as well. She decided to be the first person at work each morning. She determined to arrive early and make a fresh pot of coffee. Then as the rest of the office workers would arrive, she would offer them coffee. The workers were pleasantly surprised and genuinely grateful.

The woman would also stay after work and clean the coffee pot and cups. She would even leave a kind note to the cleaning lady as well. Soon the whole atmosphere at work changed as people became very friendly toward each other. In fact, others would come in early to make the coffee as well. Soon it became almost like a race to see who could arrive the earliest to have the privilege of making the coffee for the office. Consequently, the woman who was ready to quit was once again in love with her job. She was no longer sick of her work because she changed her own attitude and the whole work environment changed as well. She gave respect to others with a single cup of coffee. She received the respect of the entire staff in return. The words of Christ are wise words indeed: "However you want people to treat you, so treat them."

Yes my friend, respect is like a boomerang, what you give out is what you will often receive back.

Chapter 33

Loyalty Means:
Being Completely Trustworthy

Loyalty is an outstanding character quality. However, it seems that loyalty is becoming almost obsolete. Loyalty is slipping away from our society. Self-centeredness is gradually eroding away the value of loyalty. Therefore, we need people of character who understand that: Loyalty means being completely trustworthy.

I believe the very heart and soul of loyalty must be unconditional love. Jesus said in John 15:13:

Greater love has no one than this, than to lay down one's life for his friends.

Yes loyalty and sacrifice go hand in hand. Proverbs 17:17 says:

A friend loves at all times, and a brother is born for adversity.

Yes, a true friend is one who is loyal even in the midst of difficulties. In fact, loyalty is the most valuable during adversity. Sometimes a person finds out who their true friends are during the hard times. When all of the facts have not yet been revealed, people may be tempted to form permanent opinions with only partial truth. After all, the rumor mill is always ready to grind on someone's character. However, a true friend will stand shoulder to shoulder with you during the tough times.

Loyalty stands like a rock when others sink in the quick sand of quick judgment. Loyalty puts the shoulder to the wheel when others run from the work. Loyalty defends your character when others want to degrade it. Loyalty speaks up to the false critics who want to become a "lynch mob" of your character. Loyalty always gives the benefit of the doubt.

Loyalty is also compassionate when a friend has done wrong. The Scripture says in I Peter 4:8:

And above all things have fervent love for one another, for love will cover a multitude of sins.

Yes, the loyal person does not desire to see a friend who is in the wrong become destroyed. They are discreet with the disappointing news that a friend has fallen into sin. The damaging information is not spread by a friend. A true friend reaches out and helps pick up the one who is fallen.

You see, a true friend believes the best even when things go wrong. A true friend respects the other person enough to believe they will bounce back. They know that it will only make it more difficult for the person to rebuild their life if others have openly discussed the details of their faults.

Proverbs 10:12 says:

Hatred stirs up strife, but love covers all sins.

Yes, the person of hate will gladly "stir the waters" with damaging information. They will take great delight in "fanning the flames" of negative and detrimental news of someone's character flaw. They pour gas on the fire and love to watch it burn.

However, a person of love will not spread the news of sin. Love does not rejoice in iniquity, according to I Corinthians 13:6. Love does not feel the need to play the role of the "I caught you reporter." No, love may not approve of the sin, but love understands the importance of proper discretion toward the sinner.

The Scripture also instructs us concerning the importance of loving confrontation. Proverbs 27:6 says:

Faithful are the wounds of a friend, but the kisses of an enemy are deceitful.

This leads us to another important aspect of loyalty. A true friend will confront you in order to try and help you. A faithful friend will lovingly correct you in order to help you avoid an error in judgment. After all, everyone has "blind spots" in their life. Therefore, a loyal friend will confront you privately in order to help avoid public embarrassment.

My friend, loyalty is a wonderful quality. The former NFL coach Bum Phillips said this: "Loyalty, up and down the line. That's one quality an organization must have to be successful." I believe Bum Phillips was right on target. In fact, loyalty could be defined as: "the willingness to put the leader and the organization above personal desires." Loyalty is driven by the inner desire to benefit the team not the individual.

It seems that in yesterday's culture, loyalty was a premium quality. It was a compliment to be a true "company man." Today, loyalty and sacrifice are almost forgotten terms. The goals of the individual have replaced the importance of the team.

In the book, *They Call Me Coach*, John Wooden has a "pyramid of success." He has a foundational layer that has industriousness (hard work) on one corner, enthusiasm on the other corner, and loyalty right in the middle. He says that no building is any better than its structural foundation. Wooden was a firm believer in loyalty in order to be truly successful.

It's interesting to note that early in Wooden's career he desired to coach at Purdue University. In fact, after he interviewed for the job at UCLA, he was offered the job at Purdue. However, he had given a verbal commitment to go to UCLA and build a basketball program.

At that time, UCLA was a small school on the West Coast. They didn't have an established basketball program. Purdue, on the other hand, was a national basketball powerhouse. John Wooden had also graduated from Purdue and played college basketball at the University.

Now he was faced with a decision. He had given his word to the authorities at UCLA that he would accept the position as head basketball coach. They had not even drawn up the contract. They simply shook hands on it. Wooden then boarded the train and returned to South Bend, Indiana to pack his family and move to California.

When he returned to South Bend, a written offer from Purdue was awaiting him. His lifetime dream job was literally placed in his hands. The open door to his dream future was waiting for Him to walk through. However, Wooden chose to be loyal to his word. He had given his word to accept the position at UCLA. Being a man of character and remaining loyal to his word meant more than any opportunity for success. He wrote Purdue and declined their offer.

John Wooden moved to California and the rest is history. He built a basketball dynasty of his own at UCLA. It did not come overnight. He coached 20 years at UCLA before winning his first NCAA title. Then the hard work paid off. Wooden went on to win ten NCAA titles in 12 years during the 1964-1975 seasons.

I believe he was a championship coach because he was a man of championship character. Loyalty is an admirable quality. It's at the foundation of success.

By the way, we can be thankful of the loyalty of Jesus Christ toward us. Romans 5:8 says:

But God demonstrates His own love toward us, in that while we were still sinners, Christ died for us.

Yes, Jesus demonstrated the supreme act of love and loyalty when He died on the cross for our sins. Jesus was loyal to the Father's plan of salvation. You can follow Him because He is completely trustworthy. Yes, loyalty is a tremendous quality. Be loyal to God, loyal to others, and loyal to your values and you will be a person of outstanding character. Remember my friend, loyalty means being completely trustworthy.

CHAPTER 34

WE TEACH WHAT WE KNOW; WE REPRODUCE WHAT WE ARE

When it comes to influencing people, we must be genuine. We cannot motivate others to live on a level beyond what we have experienced. Basically, our true influence comes from the life we lead. In other words, our example is what rubs off on others. After all, "We teach what we know; we reproduce what we are."

Albert Schweitzer said: "Example is not the main thing in influencing others. It is the only thing." John Wooden said: "Be more concerned with your character than with your reputation. Your character is what you really are while your reputation is merely what others think you are."

Jesus said this about influencing others in Luke 6:40:

A disciple is not above his teacher, but everyone who is perfectly trained will be like his teacher.

That is why a positive relationship is extremely important with people we desire to influence. For example, children learn positive habits from parents who choose to be a positive role model. Yes, wise parents keep in mind the principle of influence, that we can teach what we know, but we only reproduce what we are.

My friend, I have discovered the value of developing positive relationships with all four of our children. I must confess that it was easy for me to bond with our three sons. It came natural for me to go outside and play football with them or come inside and "rough house" as we wrestled on the living room floor. We even enjoyed such "manly" times together like spending an evening watching a marathon of John Wayne movies.

However, I needed some help when it came to bonding with our daughter concerning the things little girls like to do. One day, I asked Cindi the question, "What can I do to spend some quality time with Hannah in order to strengthen our relationship?" Cindi smiled and said, "Have you ever thought about taking her shopping?" I gave a "sheepish grin" and admitted that it had not crossed my mind. However, I decided to give it a try.

Well, as you can imagine, we had a great time together. Hannah and I went to the mall and "shopped until we dropped." She was smiling the entire evening as we went from store to store. Most importantly, I learned how to bond with my daughter by taking an interest in something she truly enjoys.

Consequently, whenever I want to strengthen my relationship between "father and daughter", I simply take Hannah to the mall. Yes, we do a great deal of shopping, but we also spend time talking together, as well. It has helped me gain a better understanding of her life. This has given me valuable insight into ways I can demonstrate "servant leadership" and have a positive influence in the life of my daughter.

Yes, a positive example can be a powerful way to influence someone for the better. You know, Jesus was fully qualified to speak on the subject of being an influence through a life of example. After all, our Lord is the most powerful role model of all.

Jesus said in Matthew 20:26-28:

Whoever desires to become great among you, let him be your servant. And whoever desires to be first among you, let him be your slave. Just as the Son of Man did not come to be served, but to serve, and to give His life a ransom for many.

Yes, Jesus certainly led by example and was a living role model of humility and servant leadership.

Now He calls upon us to follow His example. He wants us to reveal the Christian faith through our life. We need to demonstrate the faith with a humble heart and a positive spirit. After all, we are the only Jesus that some people will ever see.

As I reflect upon someone who demonstrated the Christian life to me, I recall my favorite Sunday school teacher. Her name was Virginia Suttor and she was an outstanding Sunday school teacher. Virginia has gone home to be with the Lord, but her impact on me still lives on.

Virginia had a wonderful personality and was a tremendous Bible teacher. She taught the Word of God with great enthusiasm and creativity. The Bible stories would come alive as Virginia taught the Scriptures. It was exciting to be in her class.

Virginia was a loving teacher, but she was firm as well. In fact, she would often teach Sunday school with one hand on her Bible and the other hand on my shoulder. I was ornery and loved to "cut up", but Virginia had a way of keeping me in line.

Virginia not only taught us the Word of God, but she also introduced us to the God of the Word. Her love for the Savior was written on her face. She always taught the Bible with a smile. I have never forgotten her smiling face and her love for Christ.

She never handled the Word of God with a frown or a scowl. Even when she was firm, she always had a smile. She was the most loving Sunday school teacher I have ever known. I am convinced she played a major role in planting the Word of God in my heart.

I remember my Mom and Virginia Suttor creating some fabulous Bible School Skits. My Mom would write the script for a made up character known as "Happy." Virginia played the voice for the famous puppet and they would tell the Bible School story through "Happy." Virginia was the best person to play the part of "Happy" because she was always so happy all the time.

Most importantly, I learned that the only way to be truly "Happy" was to have Jesus in my heart. I learned that Jesus died on the cross for my sins and rose again from the dead. I learned that Jesus loves us and will fill our heart with true joy and happiness. Later on, when I was eighteen years old, I invited Christ into my life. I am convinced that the "seeds of faith" were planted in my life as a young boy through the faithful teaching of Virginia Suttor. I thank God that she reproduced the joy of Christianity in me.

My friend, "A disciple is not above his teacher, but everyone who is fully trained will be like his teacher." Yes, it is so true, "example is not the main thing in influencing others, it is the only thing." Therefore, whether you are spending a day with your child or preparing to teach a Sunday School class to other children, always remember, "we teach what we know, we reproduce what we are."

CHAPTER 35

HONESTY BUILDS TRUST
ON THE FOUNDATION OF TRUTH

The foundation of any relationship is trust. The foundation of trust is truth. Therefore, one of the most important character qualities of all is honesty. The person who is honest demonstrates a depth of character worthy of trust and admiration.

My friend, being a person of your word is a mark of maturity. Jesus said, "Let your 'yes' be 'yes' and your 'no' be 'no'." In other words, people should be able to rely upon your word. Honesty is always the best policy. After all, honesty builds trust on the foundation of truth.

The scripture says in Ephesians 4:25:

Put away all lying, each one speak truth with his neighbor, for we are members of one another."

Yes, God wants us to be people of truth. In fact, God listed lying as one of the things God hates in Proverbs 6:16-19. God says that a 'lying tongue' is an abomination to Him. Of course, the 9th commandment also forbids us from telling lies:

Thou shalt not lie.

Jesus made a very strong statement in John 8:44 when He equates lying with acting like the devil himself. Yes, make no mistake about it; the follower of Christ is to be a person of truth. Honesty reveals the strength of character that builds trust on the foundation of truth.

The opposite is also true. There is something weak in the person who cannot tell the truth. There is a deep-rooted character flaw in the dishonest person. Lies and deceit reveal an individual without a proper moral conscience.

However, the honest person understands that their word is their bond. The honest person respects others and earns their trust with truth. The honest person respects himself and doesn't try to fool the "man in the mirror." Conrad Hilton of the Hilton Hotel Corporation once said, "Some things that I have strictly adhered to are: to have integrity, to never deceive anybody, to have my word good. Under no circumstances deviate from that."

Yes, genuinely successful people understand the value of honesty. They understand that truth is the foundation of trust. Dishonesty, on the other hand, will destroy trust. Once trust has been broken, it is extremely difficult if not impossible, to reestablish.

You see this in many aspects of life. For example, a young couple will stand before a pastor and exchange their wedding vows of love and commitment. They promise to be faithful to each other until "death do they part." Those vows are a sacred commitment made in the sight of God and in the presence of other witnesses.

Then a strange thing begins to happen later on for some couples. Their vows begin to be looked upon as a conditional commitment. They decide to forget their sacred honor and go back on their word.

Perhaps someone else has caught their eye. They begin to work a little later at the office. Lies and deception begin to cover up the true motive of the heart. Then in a moment of weakness, they violate their marriage vows.

Eventually, the spouse begins to sense a shift in their relationship. A confrontation takes place and the truth is revealed. Dreams are shattered as loyalty has been exchanged for lust. Now the trust has been broken and the foundation of truth has been destroyed.

The sad reality of this takes place far too often. Dreams turn into nightmares. They drive past the church where the vows were originally given. However, now they are on their way to the courthouse to end the commitment.

The love is gone and their hearts are now "stone cold." The laughter has turned into tears. The joy has turned into sorrow. Truth has been exchanged for a lie. Devotion has given way to deception. The collapse of commitment is final and the marriage is finished.

However, God wants us to build our relationships on the foundation of truth. This will establish trust. Once trust is in place, then a relationship has great potential. Honesty is the key to building loyalty in all relationships. Honesty is always the best policy.

My friend, build your relationships on the foundation of truth. This will lay the lasting foundation of trust. Make sure you speak the truth in clear terms. Be a straightforward person. Do not "beat around the bush."

In the long run, you will build a life of great character through truthfulness. People will know they can depend on you. They will know that your words are not intended to have a "double meaning." Stay away from any form of misleading language that is intentionally designed to deceive. Be careful of exaggeration, and of course, always honor your commitments.

All of these things will enable you to build a life that is trustworthy. People will respect you because you have earned their trust. People will gladly follow your leadership and listen to your ideas. A trademark of truth will build a positive foundation of trust.

Most importantly, you will be able to look yourself in the mirror. You will not be ashamed of what you see. You will have a good sense of pride and self-respect. In fact, you will not have to look over your shoulder because you will have nothing to hide.

I'm reminded of an amazing story, as told by R. Kent Hughes, concerning a very honest young man who played high school soccer. He was considered an outstanding player and set the scoring record at his high school. However, it was his honesty that allowed him to have the greatest influence on his school and community.

In his final game, they were trailing their archrival by a score of 3-2 with less than ten seconds left to play. It looked like he would end his tremendous career with a disappointing defeat. However, he made a desperate and determined attempt to tie the game and send it into overtime. He was "cut out of the cloth" of fighting to the finish in order to "win one for the Gipper". He fired the shot just as time was expiring. He scored the tying goal and his team was ecstatic!

The event that followed was truly amazing. The referees huddled to determine if the goal was scored before time elapsed. The scoreboard clock was the official clock. No horn had sounded, but there was confusion if the clock had turned to zero before the shot.

Finally, the referee reversed the decision and took the goal away. It seems that the honest young man himself informed the officials that the time had expired. He said he glanced at the clock just before he shot and it was on the double zero.

My friend, it may have been a disappointing loss, but it was a tremendous victory. A young man had demonstrated the character of a champion. His life goes beyond the column of wins and losses. His life is built on truth. He demonstrated a trustworthiness that is worthy of great admiration. Score a great victory for moral character. Honesty builds trust on the foundation of truth.

By the way, that is exactly why you can trust God. The scripture says that it is impossible for God to lie. God always tells the truth and God always keeps His promises.

II Corinthians 1:20 says:

For all the promises of God in Him are Yes, and in Him Amen, to the glory of God through us.

Yes, you can take God at His word. Jesus died and rose again for our sins. His resurrection authenticates all of the promises in His Word. Jesus can be totally trusted because "He is the way, the truth and the life". Yes, Honesty builds trust on the foundation of truth.

CHAPTER 36

RESPONSIBILITY MEANS:
LIVING WITHOUT EXCUSES

Any successful person is a responsible person. In fact, every true leader knows the absolute importance of accepting responsibility. After all, anyone can give an excuse, but people of character understand that: responsibility means living without excuses.

The Word of God uses the illustration of following the example of an ant. It is a very small bug, but it demonstrates incredible responsibility. Proverbs 6:6-8 says:

> *Go to the ant, you sluggard! Consider her ways and be wise, which, having no captain, overseer or ruler, provides her supplies in the summer, and gathers her food in the harvest.*

The emphasis of the passage of scripture is the responsibility a little ant displays. They work hard and plan ahead. They take the responsibility of providing for their family and projecting for the future. It is an incredible lesson of being responsible and productive.

Yes, responsibility means living without excuses. Anybody can give an excuse. Reasons are always abundant as to why a job cannot be done or a commitment cannot be kept. However, people of responsibility simply refuse to make excuses. It is interesting to note that fifty years ago the emphasis was on obligations and responsibilities. Today the emphasis is on our rights and privileges. People will fight for their rights and yet walk away from responsibilities

I believe winners in life give extra effort not excuses. Vince Lombardi said, "Winning is not a sometime thing; it's an all the time thing. You don't win once in a while; you don't do the right thing once in awhile; you do them right all the time. Winning is a habit. Unfortunately, so is losing."

Yes, winners in life are "no excuses" type of people. When given a task, they follow through on their responsibility. Winners in life are people who always get the job done. People of responsibility are willing to go the extra mile. The standard of excellence is their only acceptable measuring stick.

Winners in life know the value of raising the standard to achieve success. Responsible people would never dream of lowering the bar. Leaders are responsible people who produce results regardless of the situation. They will turn a negative situation into a positive success. Bottom line, responsibility means living without excuses.

The scripture says in II Timothy 2:3:

You therefore must endure hardship as a good soldier of Jesus Christ.

Yes, a responsible person develops the mindset of a soldier. They stay at the task regardless of the challenge. They also give it everything they have regardless of feedback they receive. They embrace the mindset as found in the poem

ANYWAY
People are unreasonable, illogical, self-centered
love them anyway.
If you do good, people will accuse you of selfish, ulterior motives
do good anyway.
If you are successful, you win false friends and true enemies,
be successful anyway.
The good you do today may be forgotten tomorrow
do good anyway.
Honesty and frankness will make you vulnerable
be honest and frank anyway.

161

People love underdogs but follow only top dogs
follow some underdog anyway.
What you spend years building may be destroyed overnight
build anyway.
People really need help but may attack if you try to help
help people anyway.
If you give the world the best you have, you may get kicked in the
teeth
but give the world the best you have
ANYWAY.

Yes, responsible people give the world the best they have to offer. True success is achieving your maximum potential in the situation you are in. I fully believe that a trademark of maturity is to accept your responsibility.

Most of my friends know that I am a die hard John Wayne fan. I love to watch an old "Duke" movie. His straightforward style and "get the job done" mentality is right up my alley. The plot is simple and the message is clear. Good always triumphs over evil. In the end, right will always prevail.

One particular movie that has a clear message of responsibility is "The Cowboys." In this movie the Duke has to make a cattle drive and all his help has left. They went running after gold along the Ruby River. It comes time to move the herd to market and the Duke is without help. His back is against the wall. As a result, the Duke decides to "roll the dice" and hires several young teenage boys.

As the movie unfolds, you discover a clear message concerning the character quality of responsibility. The Duke is teaching more than herding cattle. He is teaching important life lessons along the trail. The most important lesson of all is living without excuses. Getting the job done and refusing to quit. The meaning of responsibility is loud and clear: Living without excuses.

Eventually, the group is overtaken by cattle rustlers. One of the thieves begins to slap around and rough up one of the young cowboys. The Duke has seen enough and steps forward to challenge the cattle rustler to a fistfight. After the Duke manhandles the cattle rustler, the coward shoots the Duke in the back. It was one of those rare moments when John Wayne dies in the movie.

However, the young cowboys are determined to get the herd back. The cook tells them not to pursue the men because they will all get killed. Then a classic line is given in the movie by "Slim", the leader of the teenagers. He cocks his rifle and says: "We're gonna finish the job." As a result, they recapture the herd and lead the cattle to the market.

Yes, responsibility means living without excuses. By the way, spiritual responsibility does not make excuses either. In fact, the scripture is clear that God will not accept our excuses if we reject Jesus Christ as Lord and Savior. Romans 1:20 says: "For since the creation of the world His invisible attributes are clearly seen, being understood by the things that are made, even His eternal power and Godhead, so that they are without excuse."

Yes, God says that we will not be able to give any excuses when we stand before Him. He has made it possible for us to accept Him by faith. God has revealed Himself through His Son, the Lord Jesus Christ. John 1:18 says: "No one has seen God at any time. The only begotten Son, who is in the bosom of the Father, He has declared Him."

Yes, Jesus Christ has revealed God the Father to us. Jesus went to the cross as a demonstration of the love of God. Jesus paid in full our sin debt to God when He died and rose again for us. The bodily resurrection of Christ is living proof of His victory over the grave.

My friend, Jesus offers the free gift of eternal life to all who will believe. Therefore, the responsible thing to do is invite Christ into your life by faith. Once you have trusted Christ as Savior, you can follow Him as your Lord. You will demonstrate your faith by your obedience to the Lordship of Christ.

Yes, one of the best ways to be a positive influence for the faith is following through on your responsibilities. Fulfill your commitments. Go the extra mile. Get the job done and refuse to quit. Yes, responsibility means, living with out excuses.

CHAPTER 37

LOVE IS THE
FOUNDATION FOR TRUE FRIENDSHIP

It has been said that no man is an island unto themselves. Everybody needs a friend. In fact, the best way to make a friend is to be a friend. Therefore, I want to consider the subject "Love is the foundation for true friendship."

Proverbs 17:17 says:

A friend loves at all times, and a brother is born for adversity.

Yes, a friend is someone you love unconditionally. It does not mean that you agree with everything they do. It also does not mean that you accept everything they do. However, it does mean that you choose to demonstrate your love in a positive way.

The first word that comes to my mind concerning friendship is the word "loyalty". Yes, loyalty is important in all of our relationships. True friendships will stick together through thick and thin.

By the way, a key to having a successful marriage is for the husband and wife to become great friends. This will build the foundation of loyalty and enhance the love as well. I can honestly tell you that my wife, Cindi, is my closest friend. She is the love of my life and the "wind beneath my wings." She is my greatest encourager and my partner in ministry.

Another important aspect of friendship is dependability. The scripture says, "a brother is born for adversity." In other words, true friendship is strengthened during the tough times. This may be when your friend is depending on you the most.

In fact, it is during adversity that we often find out who our true friends are. Anyone can hang around during times of great success.

However, when a big disappointment comes or a time of difficult trial, this will be a testing ground for true friendship. Who sticks around when the good times turn into bad times? Who hangs on when others are turning their backs?

Sometimes it is during the hard times when you find out who truly believes in you. The people who bail out when the ship takes on water, perhaps were never really your true friends. However, the ones who patch up the hole in the boat and grab an oar and start rowing, these are friends who were born for adversity.

I'm reminded of the friendship between Gayle Sayers and the late Brian Piccolo. The true story is beautifully told in the movie "Brian's Song."

In 1965, Gayle Sayers and Brian Piccolo were both rookies for the Chicago Bears. They were both running backs competing for the same position. Piccolo had led the nation the previous year in rushing yards and scoring while playing college football at Wake Forest. However, Gayle Sayers won the starting position for the Bears.

George Halas decided to do something very unique. He assigned Gayle Sayers and Brian Piccolo to room together. This was the first time in the history of the NFL that a black athlete shared a room with a white athlete. After all, in 1965 it was radical for these two athletes to share a room with the racial tension in our nation.

However, a beautiful friendship was developed. Sayers and Piccolo became tremendous friends on and off the field. Racial walls had been torn down and open communication was established. The two became like brothers. Their wives also became great friends in the process, as well.

The friendship also paid off for the Chicago Bears. You see, during their second season, Sayers went down with a terrible knee injury. It looked like his brilliant career would be finished. Piccolo replaced Sayers on the field and helped Sayers push himself to physical health off the field. Piccolo worked out with Sayers and constantly challenged him. Eventually the doctor gave him the OK to return to football the following season. As a result, both Sayers and Piccolo were now a winning combination in the starting back-field.

However, Brian Piccolo soon found himself fighting another battle. He was diagnosed with lung cancer at the young age of 26. Now it was Sayers' turn to motivate Piccolo to overcome the odds. Piccolo had helped Sayers fight back to football and now Sayers was helping Piccolo fight for his life.

At the end of the season, Gayle Sayers won the prestigious "George S. Halas Award." It was given to the player who was considered the most courageous. Sayers received it for the courage he displayed in fighting back from his knee injury. Every time he carried the ball during his outstanding season he ran the risk of re-injuring his knee. Now, Gayle Sayers was being rewarded at a banquet for his tremendous courage.

However, when Sayers accepted the award he began to speak of his friend, Brian Piccolo, who was in the hospital dying. He stated that Piccolo had the heart of a giant. Piccolo had rare courage as he faced his greatest opponent, cancer. Sayers stated: "You flatter me with this award, but Brian Piccolo is the man of courage. This award is mine tonight, but it will be Brian Piccolo's tomorrow." He said: "I love Brian Piccolo and I'd like all of you to love him too and tonight when you hit your knees, please ask God to love him."

There was not a dry eye in the building as Gayle Sayers sat down. The friendship between Sayers and Piccolo was an inspiration to the entire team. Piccolo lost his fight against cancer, but the world gained a shining example of true friendship. Yes, true friends love at all times and help each other out during the difficult challenges of life. Love is the foundation for true friendship.

My friend let me tell you of another friend who loves at all times. His name is Jesus Christ. The Bible says that Jesus is a friend that sticks closer than a brother. Yes, two thousand years ago, God left heaven in the person of Jesus Christ. He gave His life on the cross as a demonstration of His love for His friends, known as the human race. Jesus said in John 15:13, "Greater love has no one than this, than to lay down one's life for his friends."

Yes, Jesus Christ loves all people. In fact, He is even called the "friend of sinners." His love is unconditional. His loyalty is unforgettable. His dependability is unstoppable. Therefore, He offers to be our Savior, Lord, and the Friend who sticks closer than a brother.

My friend, do you know the "Friend who sticks closer than a brother?" Why not open your life to Jesus and meet the one who loves you and gave His life on the cross for you.

Simply invite Christ into your life as Savior and Lord. Tell Him that you believe He died and rose again for you. Jesus will give you forgiveness of sins, a home in heaven and become your friend who will love you at all times. He promises to "never leave you nor forsake you." Yes, His love is the foundation for true friendship.

CHAPTER 38

TRAVELING THE HIGH ROAD WILL REDUCE LOW LEVEL DISTRACTIONS

We all must decide which road we want to travel. We can either make our journey in life on the high road or the low road. We can be a positive influence or a negative influence. I believe you will discover that: "Traveling the high road will reduce low level distractions."

Colossians 3:1-2 says:

If then you were raised with Christ, seek those things which are above, where Christ is, sitting at the right hand of God. Set your mind on things above, not on things on the earth.

Yes, my friend, once you trust Christ as Lord and Savior, you are placed on the high road. God desires for your life to reflect a heavenly mindset. The believer is challenged to "live with eternity in view." We are to develop eternal values. This will enable us to represent Christ in a positive way on this earth.

As you seek to follow Christ, you will rise above negative distractions. Your heart will be drawn closer to the Lord and further away from destructive influences. The attitude of your heart will be directly related to the altitude of your thoughts.

I'm reminded of a story of a pilot who was flying over the Arabian Desert. He landed his plane at an oasis in order to refuel. Once he gained the much-needed fuel, he resumed his flight. Soon he was flying over a mountainous region and began to hear a strange scratching noise behind him. The pilot realized that an animal had gotten into the fuselage. He knew that the animal might gnaw away at the electrical wiring and cause a serious malfunction. Therefore, the pilot needed to solve the problem or he could be in grave danger.

He looked at the mountainous terrain and knew an emergency landing was impossible. He began to get nervous as he became painfully aware of his dangerous situation. His options were limited as he stared potential death in the face.

Then the pilot got an idea. He pulled the handle back and began climbing higher. He accelerated the plane at full throttle and began traveling higher and higher. After reaching a very high altitude, he noticed the gnawing and scratching sound had stopped.

Later, he reached his destination and made an interesting discovery. He found a huge desert rat dead in the fuselage. It seems it had crawled in unnoticed when he had refueled at the desert oasis.

The enormous desert rat died when the pilot traveled at a very high altitude. It was so accustomed to the desert climate that it could not survive the high altitude. Therefore, the quick thinking pilot had been spared from a potential tragedy. Yes, traveling the high road will eliminate low-level distractions.

My friend, the same principle is true in life. You will be so much better off if you will travel on the high road. Associate with positive people and you will be better off for it. Be a positive person and other people will enjoy your company. Do not become distracted by low-level thinking. Choose to rise above it. After all, it is such a better road to travel.

Anyone can take the low road. It is so easy to find fault with others. However, if you will look for the good, you will find it. This will enable you to be a positive influence on a negative world. People will be attracted to your positive and magnetic personality. You will be an encouragement to be around. People will be glad they had the opportunity to spend time with you. Their day will be brighter because you were a part of it.

Life on the high road begins with a smile. It is a simple gesture, yet so powerful in its effect. Smile and the world will smile back. Refuse to travel at a low level with the pack of desert rats. The negative conversation will gnaw away at your inner spirit and rob you of your energy. It will steal your joy and hold back your potential.

Negative people will gnaw and scratch away at your dreams and goals. They will shoot down a creative idea. They want everyone to wallow in the mire with them. Negative people are threatened by the positive minded and success oriented person. Therefore, they will attempt to drag you down to their low level existence.

However, positive people will lift you to higher ground. You will gain the confidence needed to achieve your goals. Positive people will influence you to pursue your dreams. You will soar with your strengths and fulfill your God given potential. Positive people will influence you toward God and encourage you in your walk with the Lord. They will help you see life through the lens of a Christ-like perspective.

Yes, set your mind on things above. Fill your mind with the Word of God and allow the Scriptures to be a "lamp to your feet and a light to your path." Focus on the promises of God and achieve the success God has planned for you. Travel the high road with positive people who will enjoy the journey with you. As you walk the high road, you will leave behind the negative distractions. James 4:8 says, "Draw near to God and He will draw near to you." Yes, the destructive forces of evil will lose their grip on you as you walk the high road.

Remember my friend; fly high and the rats cannot fly with you. Eliminate low-level distractions as you travel the high road of success.

CHAPTER 39

DEVELOP CONFIDENCE AND
IGNORE DESTRUCTIVE CRITICISM

Have you ever noticed that successful people are confident? I'm not talking about arrogant pride, but a deep seeded inner calm. It is a sense of confidence in God and His power, as well as, confidence in their own God given ability. Philippians 4:13 says:

I can do all things through Christ who strengthens me.

This type of faith is rooted in the fact that:

If God is for us, who can be against us.(Romans 8:31)

The confident person is not swayed by the crowd or by destructive criticism. This person will welcome honest feedback and even accept constructive criticism. After all, everyone can always learn to improve.

However, destructive criticism is negative and counter productive. It always tears down those who are attempting to do what the critic will not attempt. Negative critics often times complain about the way things ought to be, but never do anything about it. They interpret the world through their negative viewpoint and drag others down in the process.

Unfortunately, many people with good intentions become intimidated and throw in the towel. People who lack confidence can have their self-esteem damaged by the destructive critic. A sense of inferiority and incompetence makes people feel inadequate and so they give up. Consequently, we need to develop confidence and ignore destructive criticism.

Perhaps you have heard the story of the elderly man who was traveling from one city to another with his grandson. Their mode of transportation was a donkey. The grandfather began by allowing his grandson to ride the donkey while grandpa walked alongside.

Well, pretty soon people began to criticize. They said, "Look at the strong and healthy boy riding the donkey, while that poor old man is suffering. My goodness, it seems to me like that boy is strong enough to walk. He should let that older man ride the donkey. That boy should be ashamed of himself. What's the matter with kids these days."

Naturally, the destructive criticism began to bother them. Consequently, the grandfather and the grandson traded places. Now the older man was on the donkey and the young boy was walking. They were traveling down the road and happy to eliminate negative talk.

Well, pretty soon they came upon another group of people. Guess what? The destructive criticism started all over again. This time people said, "Would you take a look at that. A strong and healthy looking man riding on the donkey while the poor young boy is suffering. Can you believe it? How terrible of the older man to usurp his power over that poor innocent boy. That old man should be ashamed of himself."

Unfortunately, the destructive criticism began to make the grandfather feel guilty. It bothered him that people spoke of him in such a negative way. He did not want people to look down upon him. Perhaps there is a better way, he thought.

Then the grandfather got a bright idea. He and his grandson should both ride the donkey. After all, this was a "pack animal" and perfectly capable of handling the weight. Yes, this would be the perfect solution to stop the negative talk. So he invited his grandson to join him and they both gladly rode the donkey.

Well, they traveled along and everything was going fine. However, they eventually came upon another group of people and the destructive criticism began again. The people were outraged at their lack of respect for animal decency.

"Look at that," the people grumbled under their breath. "Can you believe the insensitivity of those two heavy people riding that donkey? They should be ashamed of themselves making that poor donkey suffer beneath all that weight. What is the matter with those two heartless human beings?"

Well, the grandfather once again wanted to stop the criticism. After all, he did not want to begin a "save the donkey" movement. Consequently, he decided that both of them would walk alongside the donkey. Perhaps now they would travel in peace without all the destructive criticism.

Well, as you can imagine, it was not long until the criticism began again. Soon they came to another group of people and the negative talk sprung up all over again. This time the crowd said, "Would you look at that waste. My goodness, there is a perfectly good donkey not even being used. That is ridiculous. What is the matter with those two idiots? For crying out loud, one of the two people ought to have enough sense to ride that donkey."

By now the grandfather and grandson were completely frustrated by all the criticism. It seemed that no matter what they did, people criticized them. It was completely disheartening. Finally in complete exasperation, they decided to carry the donkey on their backs! But eventually they were exhausted and never did make it to the other city. They tried to please everyone and accomplished nothing.

My friend, it is important to develop confidence and ignore destructive criticism. Otherwise, you will go through life miserable and accomplish very little. God can give you all the confidence you need. The Scripture says in Philippians 2:13:

For it is God who works in you both to will and to do for His good pleasure.

Yes, when you know Christ as your Lord and Savior, then God works in your life. You can rest assured that He has a master plan for you. You can also claim the promise that everything will work out for your good. Romans 8:28 says: "And we know that all things work together for good to those who love God, to those who are the called according to His purpose." Yes, God promises to shape the events of your life in order to draw you even closer to Him.

Jesus also gives us an understanding of the Bible in order to direct our life with eternal truth. I Peter 1:23 says:

Having been born again, not of corruptible seed but incorruptible, through the Word of God which lives and abides forever.

Yes, God gives us eternal life and then directs our life by the eternal truth of Scripture. Christ gives eternal life once we trust in Him. Then He gives eternal truth to help us follow Him. Then God promises to work in your life to enable you to live for Him. That is a formula for success that cannot go wrong. With Christ leading your life, you can develop the inner confidence to claim His promise for you. Jesus said in Matthew 19:26 that:

With men this is impossible, but with God all things are possible.

My friend, we must learn to develop confidence and ignore destructive criticism. After all, people criticized Christ Himself while He was living on this earth. People were so blinded by their negative thinking that they could not recognize the mighty works He performed. However, Jesus performed them anyway. He ignored the critics and so should you. My goodness, it was the same crowd that shouted "Hosanna" on Sunday that turned and shouted "Crucify Him" on Friday.

Yes, ignore the crowd. Have enough confidence in God to rise above the crowd. You will never eliminate criticism so don't even try. Most importantly, do not let the negative critic have a victory by discouraging you. Set your sights high, work hard, tune the critics out, and you will accomplish greatness. Yes, develop confidence and ignore destructive criticism.

CHAPTER 40

NOTHING GREAT EVER
HAPPENS ON THE OK LEVEL

There is only a fine line between the "good" and the "great." Therefore, those who achieve ultimate success begin with a standard of excellence. After all, nothing great ever happens on the OK level.

People who achieve greatness recognize that "average" is the enemy of "excellence." It has been said that average is "the best of the worst and the worst of the best." Those who lower the standard always arrive at a level of mediocrity and a spirit of apathy. However, top performers understand that raising the standard results in success.

My friend, I truly believe that God calls us to strive for excellence. Colossians 3:23 says:

And whatever you do, do it heartily, as to the Lord and not to men.

God tells us to put our whole heart into our goals. The word "heartily" implies the idea of enthusiasm. The word "enthusiasm" has an interesting origin. It comes from two words: "En" meaning "in", and "theos" meaning "God." In other words, true enthusiasm is the power of God at work in you.

When God is at work in you, then you will have the energy for excellence. You will want to glorify God in your efforts to serve Him. You will embrace the philosophy that God is not glorified in mediocrity. You will desire to achieve a standard of excellence and represent Christ in a positive way.

You will find yourself loathing the concept of average. You will want nothing to do with "the best of the worst and the worst of the best." The achievement of excellence will be the only standard that quenches your thirst for success.

I think it is important to keep in mind that God has called us to be the "light of the world." Jesus said in Matthew 5:14-16: "You are the light of the world. A city that is set on a hill cannot be hidden. Nor do they light a lamp and put it under a basket, but on a lamp stand, and it gives light to all who are in the house. Let your light so shine before men, that they may see your good works and glorify your Father in heaven."

Yes, a standard of excellence will lift you above the crowd. This will allow your light to shine brightly and illuminate a dark world. Your life will shine like a searchlight and reflect the love of Christ in a positive way. It will influence people to search for Jesus, who is the source of your strength.

People of excellence will not allow age to stop them. Many great people in history did not reach their potential until later in life. For example, Colonel Sanders was 70 years old when he discovered the value of "finger lickin good" chicken. Think about it, when most people kick back and retire, Colonel Sanders was launching an amazing career.

The Bible has some incredible stories of elderly people who accomplished great things. For example, Moses was 80 years old when he led the children of Israel out of bondage. There he was, at the ripe age of 80, telling the most powerful man in the world to "let my people go." I would say that took great courage, to say the least. Yes, Moses stood tall and strong and spoke on the Lord's behalf. The result was a tremendous success.

Let's also keep in mind the contribution of young people. For example, the Beatles were barely out of their teenage years when they changed pop music forever. Many of us still remember the Ed Sullivan show that launched the Beatles all across America. The result was a new wave of music that swept the world. Whether you like it or not: "Rock and Roll is here to stay."

The Bible also has examples of young people who achieved greatness. David was only 16 or 17 when he went after Goliath. The whole nation was frozen in fear until David stepped forward by faith. He demonstrated a calm, cool, and collected confidence in God.

His victory over Goliath has inspired many people for centuries. People have overcome incredible obstacles by following the example of David whose achievement began with his attitude of faith. David wrote in Psalm 27:1:

The Lord is my light and my salvation; Whom shall I fear?
The Lord is the strength of my life; Of whom shall I be afraid?

My friend, dare to be a dreamer. Pursue your goal will all of your heart. Refuse to live in the pack of the average. Step out of the pack and be a leader for positive change. After all, as the old saying goes, "If you are not the lead dog, the scenery never changes."

Choose to live your life with excitement and enthusiasm. Refuse to listen to the gloom and doom people. Ignore them and go forward. Remember, you will always have the small dogs nipping at your heals. Rise above them and remove the word average from your vocabulary.

Build a great marriage and develop great relationships with your kids. Work at your job with a standard of excellence. Get involved in community service and demonstrate a spirit of excellence. Choose to leave your mark on this earth by making a positive contribution to your community. After all, nothing great ever happens on the OK level.

In Northern Indiana, this principle of success is well represented by the Penn High School Football program. They have risen to an unmatched level and are literally in a league of their own. It is truly an American success story.

After all, in the early 1970's the Penn Kingsmen were actually the underdogs of high school football. It was not uncommon for

Penn to only win one or two games a season. A winning season would have been a dream come true. A conference championship was unthinkable. A state championship would have been unimaginable.

Then coach Geesman arrived on the scene. He began to build a program with a standard of excellence. All kinds of excuses could have been given as to why they could not win. However, he brought a philosophy of "no excuse football." After all, winners in life give extra effort not excuses.

Penn began working hard right from the start. It was very clear that talent would be spelled: w-o-r-k. Soon the wins outweighed the losses. In a few years they began to not only win the conference, but had become virtually unbeatable. By 1983 they had won their first state championship. In 1995, 96, and 97 they won three state championships in a row! They won a fifth state championship in the year 2000!

At the present time there are literally only a few teams in the entire state of Indiana that can even compete with Penn. They have been ranked among the national elite in high school football. Featured stories have been written about Penn in USA Today and other national press. They have even set the national record for consecutive regular season wins.

Think about it, a football program that was once a complete underdog is now the "king of the jungle." In Biblical terms, they have become the "Great Bear of the North." I believe the secret of their success goes beyond the large size of the school. Their winning tradition is found in the hearts of the players and the leadership of the coaches. Yes, the outstanding leadership of Coach Geesman and the success of Penn Football is a tremendous example of demonstrating that "nothing great ever happens on the OK level."

I believe God wants you to leave your mark on this world as well. The best way to be effective is to commit to a standard of excellence. This will help you achieve your maximum potential. You will be a tremendous influence and have a positive impact in your community.

By the way, God certainly gave you the best He had to offer. After all, II Corinthians 9:15 says:

Thanks be to God for His indescribable gift!

Yes, God offers you an incredible gift of eternal life when you trust in Christ who died and rose again for you. Believing in Christ will give you a new perspective on life as you learn to live by faith. Your standards will be raised and your goals will be achieved for the glory of God. After all, nothing great ever happens on the OK level.

CHAPTER 41

MOUNTAIN MOVING FAITH

Mountain moving faith says: "When faced with a mountain - I refuse to quit. I will walk over it or around it, but I will not walk away from it." After all, the mountain may be your opportunity to discover your miracle. Yes, the person with mountain moving faith will not throw in the towel when life tries to deliver the knockout punch. Your faith will give you the determination to grab the ropes of life and climb to your feet.

Jesus said this about mountain moving faith in Mark 11:22-24:

Have faith in God. For assuredly, I say to you, whoever says to this mountain, 'Be removed and be cast into the sea,' and does not doubt in his heart, but believes that those things he says will be done, he will have whatever he says. Therefore I say to you, whatever things you ask when you pray, believe that you receive them, and you will have them.

Yes, people of faith are not afraid to dream big. They possess the courage to attempt great things through the power of God. You see, when you dream big it will fuel your enthusiasm. Big dreams will give you special energy as you put your whole heart into the project. You will draw strength from above, which will develop your strength from within.

When you follow your dream, you will remain focused in life. In fact, often times the size of your problems is in direct proportion to the size of your dreams. When you stop dreaming, you start dying. On the other hand, when the dream is burning in your heart, you will have the vision to succeed.

The key to success is to "have faith in God." The bedrock of mountain moving faith is the unshakeable confidence in the Word of God. True success is the result of obedience to God's Word.

Joshua 1:8 says: "This Book of the Law shall not depart from your mouth, but you shall meditate in it day and night, that you may observe to do according to all that is written in it. For then you will make your way prosperous, and then you will have good success."

My friend, when you read the Bible and discover the truth of Scripture, your confidence in God will grow. God will enable you to believe the impossible. After all:

Luke 1:37 says:

with God nothing shall be impossible.

Matthew 19:26 says:

with God all things are possible.

Luke 18:27 says:

the things which are impossible with men are possible with God.

Mark 9:23 says:

If you can believe, all things are possible to him who believes

Yes, make no mistake about it. God offers you mountain moving faith. Jesus will build your faith as you study His Word. Building your life on the foundation of Scripture will strengthen your faith. The bedrock of mountain moving faith is the rock solid foundation of Scriptural truth.

However, doubt is a major barrier to mountain moving faith. Jesus says that we are not to doubt in our hearts. Doubt is like a concrete barricade to faith. Doubt will block the flow of faith and cause you to become frozen in your tracks of fear.

People who question the authority of the Word of God are often questioning the idea that God knows what is best for them. This type of doubt is a tremendous roadblock to the release of a positive faith in a loving God. In fact, the Scripture says that, "the one who doubts will be like a wave of the sea, driven and tossed by the wind."

However, let's consider some blessings from mountain moving faith. One blessing we will receive is the power to overcome obstacles. You see, mountains represent the obstacles that we face in life. Jesus makes it clear that our mountain of obstacles will be removed by faith. You can achieve great things when God and you confront a mountain.

You can remove the obstacle of guilt through faith in Jesus as your Savior. God says that, "If we confess our sins, He is faithful and just to forgive us our sins and to cleanse us from all unrighteousness." Yes, Jesus forgives and forgets. He takes our mountain of guilt and removes it from our shoulders. He conquered sin when He died for us on the greatest mountain of all: Mount Calvary. Yes, we praise God for "the old rugged cross" that stood on a "hill far away."

Another blessing of mountain moving faith will be the destruction of doubt. God will remove the mountain of doubt, disillusionment, and despair as you anchor your faith in Jesus and His Word. God will bless you with tremendous power in prayer. The roadblocks will be removed and you will have clear sailing right to the throne room of God. Your prayers will be answered through mountain moving faith.

I'm reminded of the story of the cold, snowy day in Washington DC when Air Florida Flight 90 crashed into the 14th Street bridge. The plane, baggage, and horrified passengers were suddenly tossed into the freezing water. It was a scene of panic and desperation.

A flight attendant was floundering in the icy current and striving with all her might to stay alive. Someone on shore threw her a rope but she was unable to grab it. She went under the ice-cold water and popped back up. She frantically waved her hands and desperately screamed for help. She went under a second time and stayed under much longer. She finally surfaced. Her eyes were wide open with fear as she was gasping for air. She was helplessly floundering in the freezing water. Her hopes of survival were vanishing quickly.

However, out of the debris of a tragic plane crash in the Potomac River, a real life hero was about to be born. A shy unassuming man named Vinnie Skutnick was about to emerge from complete obscurity to national fame. He was standing on the bridge watching the tragedy unfold before his eyes. Believing he could make a difference, he suddenly decided to get involved. He quickly removed his heavy overcoat, kicked off his boots, and dove into the freezing water.

Vinnie Skutnick began to swim like an Olympic champion toward the drowning flight attendant. When he reached her, he lifted her head and shoulders out of the water. Then he whispered in her ear and said: "You will live." Once he pulled her from the river, Skutnick was asked why he risked his own life to save the stranger. Vinnie Skutnick said this: "I couldn't save everybody, but I knew I could make a difference to one person."

My friend, the same will be true in your life. You may not change the world, but God will use you to make some type of lasting impact on someone. Yes, God will demonstrate His power through your mountain-moving faith.

CHAPTER 42

FAITH BELIEVES IN THE FUTURE

One key to being a positive person of faith is to believe in the future. No matter where you may find yourself today, you can confidently proclaim, "I HAVE A FUTURE." Faith has the incurable obsession to believe that: "THE BEST IS YET TO COME."

Yes, faith believes in the future.

God wants to give you confidence in your future. For example, Jeremiah 29:11 says:

For I know the thoughts that I think toward you, says the Lord, thoughts of peace and not of evil, to give you a future and a hope.

Yes, God has a future for you. God wants to energize your life with the powerful notion that God has a good plan for your life.

Psalm 84:11 says:

For the Lord God is a sun and shield; The Lord will give grace and glory; No good thing will He withhold from those who walk uprightly.

What a great promise from God for you. God promises that He will not withhold any good thing from you. The key is to have faith in God and live for Him. Faith believes in the future because positive faith is connected to the one who controls the future.

Let me tell you a story about a lady who had faith in the future. She had every reason to throw in the towel; however, she refused to quit. She chose to have faith in herself and believe that she had hope for a great future. The odds were against her, however, she courageously triumphed over the odds.

This woman wanted desperately to be an actress. However, she had some problems. She was too tall, she was too thin, and she could not act. This woman could not dance and she had no stage presence. In fact, she moved rather awkwardly on stage.

However, she had faith in the future. Her mother decided to enroll her in a good drama school. Then came a crushing blow from the director of the drama school. The director clearly and cold-heartedly told the girl's mother that drama school was a waste of good money for this untalented girl.

However, this 15-year-old girl was determined. She was stubborn and decided to pursue her career in show business. Whatever things she could not do, she determined to work hard and learn to do. This spunky 15-year-old decided she would outwork everyone. She would do whatever it took to become a success, except sacrifice the integrity of her moral character. She was determined to spell talent W-O-R-K.

She was going to rise to the top the old fashioned way. She would work herself to the bone to get there. She ignored those who told her she could not succeed. This girl had the kind of faith that believed in the future.

The next 10 years were extremely tough. She would land an occasional small part, but nothing with any real promise. The acting jobs usually paid very little and sometimes paid nothing at all.

In order to support herself in the Big Apple, she was forced to work a wide variety of odd jobs. At times she was so broke she did not even have money for a cup of coffee. However, she refused to quit and was determined to succeed. She was going to make it in show business if it killed her.

In fact, at one point it almost did kill her. She had fallen into a deep depression and considered taking her own life. She had come to a point of complete exhaustion and was unable to go on. The frantic pace was taking its toll on her body and eventually she collapsed under the pressure.

However, she refused to stop believing in herself and her God-given ability. Once her health was restored, she looked better than before and show business beckoned. With faith in the future, she confidently and boldly moved to Hollywood.

She dreamed of a chance to star in the big leagues. If only her break would happen. In the mean time, she chose to not wallow in self-pity, anger, and bitterness. She would not cultivate feelings of envy. No, not this woman. She pressed on with a positive attitude, a strong work ethic, and the faith to believe in her future.

For the next few years she slaved away in the Hollywood cellar. A small part here, a tiny part there, but nothing to really send her into stardom. However, she had the hang-on kind of faith. The word "quit" was not even in her vocabulary. When she was faced with a challenge, she simply dug in her heels and refused to quit.

Eventually, she was given a role in a movie and was finally discovered as an actress with genuine talent. Then she was given an offer on a radio show. She displayed tremendous skill as a comedian and her popularity began to grow.

Then came the invention of television. It was the break she needed and Lucille Ball was on her way to stardom. Yes, we all enjoyed that wholesome show called, "I Love Lucy."

For Lucille Ball, years of hard work had finally paid off. She had the faith to believe in her future. She rose from obscurity to a "household name." She was a woman who "kept on keeping on" even when life handed her some hard times. Lucy overcame the odds and became an enormous success.

My friend, God has a future for you, as well. God has a plan for your life. Once again Jeremiah 29:11 says:

For I know the thoughts that I think toward you, says the Lord, thoughts of peace and not of evil, to give you a future and a hope.

Yes, look to God through the eye of faith. Trust Him for the future He has for you. Accept the free gift of eternal life that Jesus so lovingly offers to you today. Follow Christ and experience your future in heaven and power for living on this earth.

Yes, faith believes in the future.

CHAPTER 43

FEED YOUR FAITH AND STARVE YOUR FEAR

It has been said that we are what we eat. That is certainly true in the physical realm. Our body will directly reflect the kinds of foods we have been eating. It is nearly impossible to hide.

It is also true in the emotional aspect of our life. We reflect, by our emotions, what we have been feeding our mind. If we feed our minds with positive thoughts, we will have a pleasant disposition. However, if we focus on negative or depressing ideas, our emotions will sink into the valley. We may find ourselves "down in the dumps."

It is also true that we are what we eat spiritually, as well. Jeremiah 15:16 says:

Your words were found, and I ate them, And Your word was to me the joy and rejoicing of my heart; For I am called by Your name, O Lord God of hosts.

Therefore, feed your faith and starve your fear.

It has been said that every person has two dogs living inside of him. We have a good dog and a bad dog, and the one you feed is the one that will grow. We could say we have a dog of faith and a dog of fear living inside us. You feed the dog of faith and your courage will grow. You will be energized and excited to move forward.

Jesus spoke of the importance of developing mountain moving faith in Matthew 17:20.

Jesus said, 'If you have faith as a mustard seed, you will say to this mountain, move from here to there', and it will move, and nothing will be impossible for you.

This faith gives us the courage to tackle the impossible. Yes, great things happen when you feed your faith and face your mountain.

However, sometimes we unknowingly feed the dog of fear. We begin to focus on what could go wrong. We look at the world and wonder if evil will triumph over good. Are the best days behind us and the worst days in front of us? We ask the same question Merle Haggard sang about in his country song, "Are the good times really over for good?"

Consequently, a growing spirit of anxiety begins to develop. The dog of fear begins to take control of our life. This fear begins to spin out of control. We feel a sense of hopelessness as worry bulldozes through our heart. Our mind is gripped with doubts and our body is frozen by fear.

The solution is to feed your faith and starve your fear. Jesus wants us to secure our faith in Him because He is the rock of our salvation. The Scripture says in Psalm 62:6:

"He only is my rock and my salvation; He is my defense; I shall not be moved."

Yes, Jesus is our rock that does not roll. After all, when your feet are planted on the rock of Jesus Christ, then your heart will be unmovable and unshakeable. Fear will have no grip on you. Faith will be your guide and your power source.

The Scripture says in II Timothy 1:7, "For God has not given us a Spirit of fear, but of power and of love and of a sound mind." Yes, God will not give you a spirit of fear. God will enable you to advance with boldness. He will fill your heart with courage as your faith is focused on God.

David cried out in Psalm 27:1:

The Lord is my light and my salvation; Whom shall I fear?
The Lord is the strength of my life; Of whom shall I be
afraid?

David was certainly qualified to write those words. After all, he fed his faith and starved his fear. The result was slaying the giant, Goliath. He moved forward by faith and looked fear straight in the eye. His faith enabled him to cast his mountain into the sea. Nothing was impossible for David when he exercised mountain-moving faith.

I'm also reminded of the story of a man who wanted to cross the frozen St. Lawrence River in Canada. It was in the dead of winter and the river had frozen solid. It had been a very harsh winter and the arctic weather had taken its course.

However, this man was still fearful of crossing the frozen river. He was not convinced that the river was completely frozen over. Perhaps it was not totally frozen. What if he fell through the ice? What if he was too heavy and the ice could not hold him? One wrong move and it might cost him his life.

The man knelt down and placed his hand on the ice. He pushed down to see if the ice might break. Then he crawled out onto the ice. He began to move very slowly and exercised extreme caution. Eventually, he made it to the center of the river. He was still down on all fours as he trembled with fear.

His heart was pounding with fear at the thought of breaking through. He thought of his wife and children. How would they get along if the ice gave way and he perished? His mind was racing wildly as the fear and anxiety nearly overwhelmed him. The man felt like his heart would beat right out of his chest.

He became short of breath from all the fear. He began to question his wisdom for venturing out onto the ice. There he was in the middle of a frozen river. He was too far out to turn back and too afraid to go on. He was literally frozen by fear.

Suddenly, he heard the noise of an approaching wagon being pulled by horses. The man driving the wagon was moving rapidly upon the frozen river. The horses were galloping along as they pulled the wagon with great power.

When the wagon reached the river, the horses did not even slow down. The driver cracked the whip and they kept right on moving. The heavy wagon and the huge horses journeyed right onto the frozen river. The man driving the wagon and team of horses waved as they boldly crossed the river.

The wagon sped right past the man crawling on the ice. The wagon driver shouted out that it was perfectly safe to cross. He had been driving his team of horses across the frozen river for a few weeks. Winter was well in place and the river was frozen solid as a rock.

You see my friend; one man inched along because he fed his fear. The other man moved along boldly because he fed his faith and starved his fear. His faith had an object that was rock solid. He had tested the ice and knew it was dependable. He moved with confidence and had complete peace of mind.

The same is true in our relationship with God. We can either inch along or we can move forward boldly. Either way, Jesus is going to hold us up. The question is simply-In what way do you want to travel? Do you want doubt and fear to freeze you with anxiety or do you want to trust God and have total peace of mind?

The Scripture says in Hebrews 11:6:

But without faith it is impossible to please Him, for he who comes to God must believe that He is, and that He is a rewarder of those who diligently seek Him.

Yes, God rewards those who approach Him by faith. God is pleased when we anchor our faith in Jesus, who died and rose again for our sins. God will give you confidence as you live by faith. Therefore, feed your faith and starve your fear.

CHAPTER 44

YOUR ATTITUDE
DETERMINES YOUR ALTITUDE

It has been said that success does not come through the way you think it comes; it comes through the way you think. Often times, the fine line between a victory and defeat lies in our attitude. Thomas Jefferson said, "Nothing can stop the man with the right mental attitude from achieving his goals; nothing on earth can help the man with the wrong mental attitude." Yes it is so true, "your attitude determines your altitude."

You know the Bible gives some benefits from focusing on life with a positive attitude. Philippians 4:8 says:

Finally, brethren, whatever things are true, whatever things are noble, whatever things are just, whatever things are pure, whatever things are lovely, whatever things are of good report, if there is any virtue and if there is anything praiseworthy-meditate on these things.

Yes, God wants you to think on good and noble things. In essence, God is saying look for the good and you will find it. That's why Hebrews 12:2 encourages us to focus our minds on Jesus Christ. The Scripture says:

Looking unto Jesus, the author and finisher of our faith, who for the joy that was set before Him endured the cross, despising the shame, and has sat down at the right hand of the throne of God.

Yes, your attitude will cause your altitude to rise like the wind as you focus your mind on Jesus Christ. Think about it, the

Almighty God of this universe loved you enough to send His Son to the cross for your sins. Jesus Christ voluntarily sacrificed His life to give you eternal life. That my friend is good news worth meditating on.

Another value of a positive attitude is found in the fact that you will be a blessing to others. Proverbs 12:25 says, "Anxiety in the heart of man causes depression, But a good word makes it glad." Yes, a kind word can pick people up and motivate them to go on. Your attitude will not only determine your own altitude, but you will help others soar to new heights as well.

Another benefit of a positive attitude is found in the value of focusing your mind on God's faithfulness. This will give you the power to persevere during the challenging times of life. Lamentations 3:22-24 says:

Through the Lord's mercies we are not consumed, because His compassion's fail not. They are new every morning; Great is Your faithfulness. The Lord is my portion, says my soul, Therefore I hope in Him.

Yes, trust in God and never give up. Keep a positive mindset. Keep your eyes fixed on God and refuse to let negative thinking creep in. Determine to bounce back from any difficulty. Determine to be a part of the answer and refuse to be a part of the problem. Determine to follow the path of success with a positive mental attitude. Let your attitude determine your altitude.

In 1956, Don Larsen was pitching for the New York Yankees. He was considered a mediocre pitcher, who had helped lead his team to the World Series against the Brooklyn Dodgers. It was fierce backyard rivalry.

In the second inning of the second game the Dodgers bats exploded. They literally knocked Larsen off the mound in two innings. Larsen had blown a six run Yankee lead in only two innings. The Dodgers won the game, but the Yankee pitcher refused to get down on himself.

Four days later he was scheduled to pitch again. Due to Larsen's lack of pitching success, most people thought the manager should start someone else. The common joke about Larsen was: "The only difference between Larson and the Titanic was that it took the Titanic longer to sink."

Many people felt that Larsen should be released from the team. However, Larsen changed the minds of the skeptics on October 8, 1956, in the fifth game of the World Series. Amazingly enough, Casey Stengel gave the nod for Don Larsen to start on the mound. The manager told Larsen the day before that he would start in game five of the World Series.

Don Larsen responded with a simple but confident statement. He said, "I'm going to beat those guys tomorrow." What took place next literally became baseball history. Don Larsen achieved what had previously never been accomplished in a World Series game. He pitched a perfect game! It was previously considered unthinkable and impossible!

However, Don Larsen did what no one had ever done before in the World Series. He only faced 27 batters and shut down the opponent with 27 consecutive outs. No one even reached first base. It was the greatest pitching performance in the history of baseball.

The Yankee Stadium was packed with 129,038 fans that witnessed a miracle in the making. When the final out was made, Yogi Berra, the team catcher, sprinted to the mound and leaped into the arms of Don Larsen. Pandemonium cut loose at Yankee Stadium as the fans went wild with celebration.

Think about it, just four days prior, Larsen had been knocked off the mound in two innings. Now he had achieved what no other major league pitcher had done before. Don Larsen overcame a million to one odds as he made history and pitched the perfect game in World Series competition. Yes, his attitude determined his altitude.

My friend, what are your dreams? What are your goals that others might think are impossible? Let me encourage you to fill your mind with the Word of God and surround yourself with positive people. This will develop your faith and give you the confidence to go for it!

CHAPTER 45

THE GUIDING LIGHT

Basically, we have two choices in life. We can either live by our own human instincts or we can follow the teachings of Jesus and the Word of God. Psalm 119:105 says:

Your Word is a lamp unto my feet and a light unto my path.

God says His Word is available to give us a light along the path of life. Jesus offers to be our guide and show the way that leads to eternal life. Yes, the Bible is the guiding light.

I remember going to Wyandotte Cave as a little boy. We were taking a family vacation and everyone was very excited. We left early on a Saturday morning and headed for Southern Indiana. The whole family piled into the car and off we went. It was the kind of weekend when life-long family memories are made. It was a rare treat to be on vacation and everyone anticipated the family outing.

Once we got to Wyandotte Cave, we signed up for one of the Cave Tours. We had a tour guide with a lantern to lead the way. I was only five or six years old, but I remember it like it was yesterday. Touring the cave was exciting and adventuresome. I'm sure my mind raced as my imagination ran wild in the cave.

At one point, the tour guide shut off his lantern to show us how dark the cave really was. I remember that you could not even see the hand in front of your face. It was pitch black without the lantern. I was glad when the guide re-lit the lantern and led us out of the cave. We would have been totally in the dark and helpless without our guide and his lantern. He was truly our "guiding light."

That is exactly why God gave us His Word. "It is a lamp to our feet and a light to our path." In other words, the Bible shines light to navigate us through a world of darkness. Yes, life without God is truly a life of darkness. However, life with the guidance of God's Word gives us meaning and purpose.

The theme of the entire 119th Psalm is the Word of God. In fact, we see several things that the Word of God will do for you as your "guiding light." We discover that it will cleanse you from sin. Psalm 119:9 says:

How can a young man cleanse his way? By taking heed according to Your Word.

It will also protect you from falling into sin. Psalm 119:11 says:

Your Word I have hidden in my heart, That I might not sin against You.

Yes, the Bible will instruct you concerning "right" and "wrong." The purpose of the instruction is to help you avoid the mistakes of life that bring pain and sorrow. After all, God knows what is best for you and He will always lead you in the right direction.

Next, we see that Scripture will strengthen your life. Psalm 119:28 says:

My soul melts from heaviness; Strengthen me according to Your Word.

Yes, sometimes we all need strength for the journey. We need a fresh dose of power for living. Well, this strength is found in the Word of God.

The Scripture is also said to give you life. Psalm 119:50 says:

This is my comfort in my affliction, For Your Word has given me life.

Yes, the love of God that flows from the Word of God will bring health and healing to your soul. Jesus said in John 6:63 that "the words that I speak to you are spirit, and they are life."

My friend, the Word of God is of priceless value to your life. Psalm 119:72 says:

The law of Your mouth is better to me than thousands of coins of gold and silver.

Yes, the Word of God is extremely valuable because it shows you more than how to make a living. The Scriptures show you how to live. Remember, *the Bible is not a rulebook to make you miserable; it is a roadmap to make you successful.*

The Scripture is indestructible because it is eternal. Psalm 119:89 says:

Forever, O Lord, Your Word is settled in heaven.

As the old saying goes, "God said it, I believe it, and that settles it with me." Yes, the Bible is the eternal Word of an eternal God.

The Bible has an amazing continuity. The Bible is a collection of 66 books written over a period of 1600 years by 40 different authors with diverse backgrounds, yet the Bible has one central theme, Jesus Christ. That my friend is a book you can depend on.

The Word of God is also our delight, according to Psalm 119:92. In fact, the prophet Jeremiah was known as the "weeping prophet." He faced many challenges and trials. His life was filled with heartbreak and disappointment. Yet, he said in Jeremiah 15:16 that the Word of God was to him the "joy and the rejoicing of his heart." Yes, you can find joy in God's Word.

Last but not least, we know that the Bible is the truth. Psalm 119:160 says:

The entirety of Your Word is truth, and every one of Your righteous judgments endures forever.

Yes, the Bible is truth from cover to cover. After all, it is the divinely inspired Word of the Living God. My friend, God did not inspire a book of fables. It is truth that you can build your life on. The Bible is eternal truth, which makes it relevant for every generation. That is exactly why you can trust the Word of God to be your guiding light.

You know, just as my parents took me on a trip to Wyandotte Cave, we also took our children to the cave as well. Cindi and I had the delight of going on a Cave Tour when our four children were younger. It was over 30 years after the time I went as a boy, but the tour was the same. The cave was just as dark when they turned off the light. Nothing had changed. Fortunately, the light was just as bright when they turned it back on.

The same is true with the Word of God. The world may seem dark, but the Word of God is the "guiding light" for every generation. The Bible is the eternal truth and relevant for every generation.

Yes, the Word of God is "a lamp unto our feet and a light unto our path." Just as we had a guide through Wyandotte Cave with a light to show the way, so the Bible is our guide to direct us to Jesus and navigate our life here on earth. Don't sit in the dark. Follow Jesus and allow His Word to be your guiding light.

CHAPTER 46

JESUS IS THE
ROCK SOLID FOUNDATION

Faith in Christ is building your life on solid ground. Jesus said in Matthew 7:24-27:

Therefore whoever hears these sayings of Mine, and does them, I will liken him to a wise man who built his house on the rock. And the rain descended, the floods came, and the winds blew and beat on that house; and it did not fall, for it was founded on the rock. But everyone who hears these sayings of Mine, and does not do them, will be like a foolish man who built his house on the sand: and the rain descended, the floods came, and the winds blew and beat on that house; and it fell. And great was its fall.

Yes, Jesus is the Rock Solid Foundation.

I remember one of my favorite books as a little boy. It was *Toby and His Beachhouse*. My late Aunt Elma gave the book to me. She was a Godly woman who prayed for all of her nieces and nephews. Every year she also sent us a present with spiritual value for our birthday.

One year she gave me the book, *Toby and His Beachhouse*. It was the story of a little boy who tried to build a little playhouse on the beach. However, every evening the tide would sweep the house away.

Finally, he went and visited his uncle and explained his problem. His uncle showed Toby how to put a foundation under the house. This enabled the house to stand firm against the tide. The wise uncle also explained how we are to build our life on Christ. This will keep our life together during the storms of life. The waves and turmoil of life will beat against Christ and He will see us through.

Yes, Jesus is a Rock Solid Foundation. He tells us that if we hear His sayings and do them, we will be wise. However, the foolish person ignores the teaching of Christ and does his own thing. The foolish person has the attitude of "I'll live my life my way." However, when the storms of life begin to blow, then the house on the sand comes tumbling down.

You see, there are some similarities and differences in the builders. Both built a house because they wanted a place of refuge. Both heard the instruction of the Word of God. However, one heard and obeyed, but the other heard the Word and ignored it. Consequently, one had a foundation to uphold his life and stand the test of time. However, the other lacked the stability to endure the storms of life.

Our Lord is teaching the importance of obeying the Word of God. Therefore, God includes a promise of blessing to those who follow the teachings of Christ. God says there will be a foundation to our faith. We will have something to build our life on. That something is a someone. Jesus is the Rock Solid Foundation.

You know, growing up in a bricklayer's home taught me the importance of a good foundation. My dad was a bricklayer and every summer my brothers and I would work for dad. We mixed mortar, carried bricks, raked joints and set up the skaffle. Our job was to keep dad and his crew of bricklayers in steady supply of bricks and mortar.

I remember how frustrated dad would get if the concrete footings had been poorly done. It made his job much harder. The foundation was crucial for a proper home. It took extra work to overcome a poor foundation.

However, when the foundation was right, the bricks went on the wall with ease. The men could tackle the job more quickly and certainly more smoothly. The atmosphere on the job was always better when the foundation was right.

My friend, the same is true in life. Jesus wants our life to have a solid foundation. He wants us to build our life on the Word of God and faith in Christ. He wants us to demonstrate our faith by obeying the Lord. This causes our relationship with Christ to grow stronger. When the problems come, and they will, Jesus upholds us and becomes our "rock solid" foundation.

It is interesting to note that there are also similarities and differences of the buildings in this passage as well. Both buildings look the same. Both houses face a storm. However, there was one key difference. One house had a foundation, but the other house did not have a foundation. Therefore, one house stood firm while the other fell to the ground.

You see my friend; it is not a question as to whether we will have any problems. The question is this: "Who or what will we look to in order to get through a problem? Will we depend on our own wisdom or will we look to Jesus Christ? Will we depend on the Word of the living God or simply live by our own wits?"

My friend, Jesus is the Rock Solid Foundation. Ephesians 2:20 calls Him "the chief cornerstone." Yes, the Scripture is clear, Jesus is the only dependable foundation to hold our life together. Nothing can shake you when you build your life on Christ.

Consequently, we see the major breakpoint. One house withstands the pressure. This house has the rock solid foundation of faith in Jesus Christ. This house does not fall because it is built on the Rock. The storm beats against the Rock. Therefore, Jesus shields this person from danger.

However, the other life is built on sinking sand. Once the storm hits, this person falls apart. This is a life without Christ and without the direction of the Word of God. Eventually, it hits a break point and falls apart because the pressure is simply too much.

My friend, we need to take note of something. We must understand that God uses storms and challenges of life to reveal our foundation or lack of one. Hardships will reveal whether our faith is anchored to Christ or drifting at sea. Often times, it takes pressure to reveal what we are made of. After all, a crisis does not mold our character it simply reveals it. If we build our faith on Jesus Christ and obedience to the Word of God, we will hold up under pressure.

However, no matter how much it may appear that we have it all together, if we are not building our life on Christ, it will eventually be revealed. Once a big enough storm begins to blow, your life will collapse if there is not the proper foundation. The pressure will be too much and it will take its toll. The veneer of our life will peel away and expose what we are truly made of.

I'm reminded of the story of the late Dr. Joseph Parker. He faithfully proclaimed the Word of God for years as he pastored the historic City Temple in London. Countless men and women came to Christ from his Biblical preaching.

However, he began to listen to liberal theologians who denied the Word of God. They said the Bible was no longer relevant. People were being enlightened into more educated ways of thinking.

Dr. Parker began to mingle with these men at various conferences. They would devalue the preaching of the Word of God. In time, their influence began to take a toll on him. He began to doubt the Word of God and his faith began to slip. Consequently, his preaching took on a different dimension with less scripture and more "modern thought."

Then his beloved wife of many years became sick and died. His heart was shattered. He was a broken man and overwhelmed by grief. He sought comfort in modern theology. However, he found no comfort in a Bible torn to shreds by modern thought and the powerless God of modern theology.

Then the aged preacher returned to the gospel of redemption through the blood of Christ. He returned to the message of the death, burial and resurrection of Christ for our sins. He placed his feet down on the Word of God and rediscovered the rock solid foundation. He stated, "He would die resting upon that blessed glorious truth of salvation through the precious blood of Christ."

My friend, follow Christ and build your life on His Word. After all, you cannot go wrong because your life will have a foundation to withstand the storms of life and the strength to persevere the trials of life. Yes, Jesus is the Rock Solid Foundation.

CHAPTER 47

BELIEVING IS SEEING

Some people say, "I'll believe it when I see it." In other words, for them: "seeing is believing." They like to have something proven to them instead of accepting something by faith. After all, they do not want to be played for a fool. However, the Scripture says in Hebrews 11:1:

Now faith is the substance of things hoped for, the evidence of things not seen.

Yes, the person of faith understands that believing is seeing.

In fact, sometimes we must believe in order to see. For example, several years ago a house caught on fire in a small Midwestern farming community. The house was a two-story house that belonged to a young family. Flames swept through the house as the young family scrambled for safety.

They made their way through the smoke filled house and gathered on the front lawn. The parent's hearts sank as they realized their five-year-old son was trapped inside the blazing house. The father looked up and saw the boy crying at his bedroom window. The boy was rubbing his little eyes and crying for help.

The father knew he could not re-enter the house and survive in the raging fire. Smoke was pouring through the house as time was quickly running short. The father stood on the ground below the window and shouted for his boy to jump. The father desperately pleaded for the little boy to jump to safety. The father screamed at the top of his lungs "Jump son! I'll catch you."

The little boy was sobbing and fear was gripping his heart. He stood there frozen with fear and frightened beyond imagination. The father cried out again with a frantic plea, "Jump son! I promise I will catch you." The little boy cried out and said "but I can't see you daddy." The father answered with great assurance, "No you can't, but I can see you. Please jump and I will catch you son."

Finally, the little boy jumped and his father caught him. The boy was safe in the arms of his father. Once he jumped through the smoke his dad caught him as he promised. The little boy had to believe in order to see. He trusted his father even though he could not see him through the smoke and fire. The boy took his father at his word and took a "leap of faith." The result was safety and security in the strong and loving arms of the father.

My friend, in some ways our relationship with God is a calculated "leap of faith." We cannot understand everything there is to know about God. However, we must trust in His Word and leap into the arms of God. The good news is the fact that God is always there to protect us.

You know, Jesus offers a special blessing to those who "have not seen and yet believed." After our Lord had resurrected from the dead, He appeared to His disciples. However, Thomas was not present at the time of Christ's appearance. Consequently, Thomas refused to believe that Jesus had risen from the dead. Thomas said to the other disciples, "Unless I see in His hands the print of the nails, and put my finger into the print of the nails, and put my hand into His side, I will not believe."

Thomas was saying that for him, seeing would be believing. He refused to believe unless he saw the Lord with his own eyes and touched the Lord with his own hands. In other words, prove it and I will believe it. Eventually, Jesus appeared to Thomas and he went from a doubter to a believer.

My friend, believing is seeing. Psalm 119:18 says:

Open my eyes, that I may see wondrous things from Your law.

Yes, God will reveal Himself in a magnificent way to those who believe in Him and trust in His Word. In fact, it has been said that

"A Bible which is falling apart usually belongs to someone who is not."

My friend, we live in a cynical and skeptical world. Unfortunately, many believe that the Word of God is no longer relevant today. Modern culture says we want new ideas and new values. We don't want moral absolutes to govern our life.

Often times, people say the old values no longer apply to our life today. Some say they would believe if it could be proven that Jesus is the eternal Son of God and the Scriptures are the true Word of God. For these people: Seeing is believing.

However, God responds back to us that: "Believing is seeing." It is only after we place our faith in Christ as Lord and Savior that we can see the beauty of a relationship with Christ. Once we accept by faith the death, burial, and resurrection of Christ as the sacrifice for our sins, we begin to discover the incredible promises God has for us.

Our eyes become open to scripture and we can understand spiritual truth like never before. We learn the reality of the words of Jesus when He said in John 8:32, "You shall know the truth and the truth shall set you free." That is also why Jesus said in John 8:36, "Therefore if the Son makes you free, you shall be free indeed."

My friend, Jesus told us that blessed are those who have not seen and yet believe. He went on to say in John 20:31, "But these are written that you may believe that Jesus is the Christ, the Son of God, and that believing you may have life in His name."

In other words, God has given us enough knowledge to believe on Christ. Our Lord died on the cross for our sins. He gave His life as a sacrifice for our sins. He shed His blood on the cross to pay in full the penalty for our sins. Jesus rose again from the dead as living proof of His victory over sin, Satan, and hell itself. Consequently, faith in Christ allows us to experience a personal relationship with God.

My friend, you may feel like the smoke from the trials of life is blocking your view of God. You may feel like you are trapped in the fire of personal pressure and the pain of disappointing circumstances. You may desire to believe in God and yet you wonder if he really cares for you.

Yes, Jesus cares for you. His arms are open wide for you to leap from the window of doubt. Jesus is waiting for you and will catch you as you take your "leap of faith." You will find security and safety in the strong arms of Jesus. You will discover that believing is seeing.

CHAPTER 48

CHOOSE YOUR WEALTH WISELY

How do you determine your wealth? Do you simply look at your bank account? Are money and material possessions what make you tick? Some people have such a strong desire for monetary wealth that they are willing to sacrifice their values to get ahead. However, you must learn to: choose your wealth wisely.

George Washington said this: "Few men have virtue to withstand the highest bidder." In other words, most people have their price. If the bid is high enough, eventually they sacrifice their principles to increase their pay.

However, Jesus said in Mark 8:36:

For what will it profit a man if he gains the whole world, and loses his own soul?

Yes, everyone must answer the question asked by our Lord. After all, what good will it do to have all the things money can buy, and yet lose your soul? You have heard of being "dollar wise and penny foolish." Well, this is being earthly wise and eternally foolish.

Jesus went on to say in Mark 8:37

Or what will a man give in exchange for his soul?

In other words, if we pursue life without thought of our relationship with God, we make a very foolish exchange. This is an exchange rate that is foolish in anybody's books.

Yes, Jesus asked the most important question in the world. What will it profit a man if he gains the whole world and loses his own soul? Or what will a man give in exchange for his soul? In other words, choose your wealth wisely.

You know, I'm reminded of one of the all time great basketball players. His name is David Thompson. His talent matched the great players like Kareem Abdul Jabbar, Larry Bird, Wilt Chamberlain, Magic Johnson, and Michael Jordan. Yes, David Thompson had that kind of talent.

His leaping ability was out of this world. He had a vertical jump of 42 inches. Even though he was only 6' 4," he could rebound with the best of ball players. You could put a dime on the top of the backboard and David Thompson could leap up and retrieve it. His leaping ability was incredible. They called him the Sky Walker. In fact, he could slam-dunk a basketball in the eighth grade when he was only 5'8". No wonder he became a superstar!

David Thompson went to North Carolina State and played college basketball. Going into the 1974 NCAA Tournament the North Carolina State Wolfpack was ranked number one and the UCLA Bruins were ranked number two. Incidentally, North Carolina State's only loss was a regular season loss to UCLA by a score of 84-66.

The rematch with UCLA was set for the final four. The showdown between David Thompson and players like Keith Wilks and Bill Walton was scheduled. Thompson led his team to an 80-77 victory. Then they polished off Marquette to earn the national championship!

Later, David was drafted to the pros. Twice he was selected first team allstars. He was named the NBA most valuable player in 1979. He had been the college player of the year in 1975 and just four short years later was the NBA player of the year. Once he scored 73 points against the Detroit Pistons. It was a scoring performance that is remembered still. David Thompson was on his way to superstardome. He had it all!

However, bad habits began to creep in. His drinking was getting out of control. Eventually, he was introduced to drugs such as cocaine, which began to ruin his life. The excuses began to mount as he started missing practices and even games.

Eventually, while on a road trip to New York, disaster would happen. After the game, he went to Studio 54 with some of his friends. David was partying at the nightclub, and his career would come crashing down. He was pushed down some steps and suffered a knee injury that ended his career. While he is one of the greatest to play the game, his career was cut short by unwise decisions.

Thompson was devastated. Then, the IRS stepped in and investigated some bad investments. They took his million-dollar dream home in Denver, his four level condominium in Seattle, his Rolls Royce, Porsche, and Mercedes.

The disappointment was overwhelming. The pressure also affected his home life and everything began to collapse. Eventually, David Thompson was broke and lost his entire wealth and fame. In fact, he was even sent to jail for six months.

However, what was an earthly disaster turned into a heavenly miracle. David Thompson turned his life over to Christ while in jail. He cried out to God and invited Christ into his life as Lord and Savior.

God put David's life and marriage back together. He went on to become the youth program director for the Charlotte Hornets. He has been quoted as saying, "I've learned that the Lord Jesus Christ should always be your number one priority. I don't have the wealth and fame I once had, but in a lot of ways my life is far richer than it has ever been because I've got Christ in my life." In other words, David Thompson has discovered the true wealth in life.

My friend, Jesus loves you today. He died on the cross for your sins and rose again the third day proving that His sacrifice on the cross completely satisfied God the Father. Now, Jesus offers the free gift of eternal life to anyone who will believe. He asks the most legitimate question of all time: "What will it profit a man if he gains the whole world, and loses his own soul?" Yes, choose your wealth wisely.

CHAPTER 49

JESUS OFFERS YOU
A TREMENDOUS LIFE

What is your view of the Christian life? Many people have the idea that God will make them miserable as a Christian. I must confess that some Christians do not advertise the faith in a positive way. Too many mope around with that, "I'm just suffering for Jesus look." Toss in a negative critical spirit and you a have a real winner! My goodness, it's no wonder some people shy away from the faith.

However, Jesus offers you a tremendous life. After all, Jesus said in John 10:10:

The thief does not come excep to steal, and to kill, and to destroy. I have come that they may have life, and that they may have it more abundantly.

Yes, Jesus offers you a rich and meaningful life. Jesus says that He has come to give you a life that overflows with His abundance.

The word "abundantly" in John 10:10 is rich in meaning for the believer. The word gives the idea of that which supersedes just a mere existence. It is the idea of experiencing far above and beyond a normal life. It is a life filled with unspeakable joy. Even in the midst of challenges, there is joy in knowing Jesus.

Notice what Jesus calls the devil in John 10:10. He calls him the "thief." No one likes a thief. A thief is driven by selfish motives and does not care about anyone else. A thief can enter a house and take precious treasures from people and never lose a minute of sleep. Yes, a thief has no conscience.

My friend, the devil himself wants to rob you of the good life. He wants you to stay bound by insecurity and fear. He wants you to live in fear instead of faith. The devil loves to steal your mind with a negative attitude.

Yes, that is how the devil operates. He does not care about you. He isn't concerned about your future. He does not care if you throw your life away. In fact, he wants to steal your dreams and goals. He wants to take away your happiness. He wants to rob you of all true joy.

Jesus, on the other hand, wants to give you good things. He offers a life of meaning and value. He will give you a life that supersedes anything you could ever imagine. Yes, Jesus offers you a tremendous life.

My friend, before I trusted Christ as Savior, I used to think that the Christian life would be a miserable experience. I was hesitant to follow Christ out of fear that life would be dull and boring. Going to heaven sounded very good, but the life on earth did not look very exciting. However, nothing could be further from the truth.

I have discovered that Jesus gives us a tremendous life. God has blessed my life in many ways. He has given me a wonderful family. My wife, Cindi, and our four children are truly a gift from God.

I believe the Lord brought Cindi and I together for the purpose of experiencing the abundant life that Jesus offers. Her influence has helped me discover true joy and contentment in life. She has taught me to celebrate the goodness of God and His many blessings on our family. She has brought a balance to my life and taught me to take the time to enjoy our accomplishments.

One of the special things she does to help our family celebrate the goodness of God is her "blue plate award." Cindi will often times set a special blue plate on the dinner table in honor of one of the family members. The person with the blue plate as their table setting is always recognized for a particular achievement.

We have celebrated all kinds of special events such as: athletic accomplishments, academic achievements, cheerleading awards, birthdays, anniversaries, Mother's Day, Father's Day, etc. We also include the celebration of "spiritual highlights" to reinforce spiritual values. We even recognize special character qualities to help develop "championship character" in our family.

It is a loving touch that adds a very positive dimension to the special occasions. It builds positive self-esteem as she helps each family member feel special. It also helps everyone celebrate the blessings of God on our entire family as we honor each individual.

I can truly say that I thank God for the tremendous life He has given us together. I am glad to discover that the Christian faith is a positive experience filled with inner joy that only God can provide. Yes, Jesus came to this earth to give us a tremendous life as we follow Him.

My friend, Jesus offers you an abundant life, as well. The enemy wants to rob you of your dreams and goals. However, Jesus will give you the wisdom to go beyond your wildest dreams. He died and rose again to be your personal Lord and Savior. He offers to live in you and empower your life. Yes, Jesus offers you a tremendous life.

CHAPTER 50

BELIEVE IT AND YOU WILL RECEIVE IT

Perhaps you have heard the motivational phrase, "Believe it and you will achieve it." There is a great concept in that idea. It is true that we often achieve things in life that we truly believe we can accomplish. Jesus said in Mark 9:23:

If you can believe, all things are possible to him who believes.

Yes, the human mind is the big key to accomplishing great things. I trust you have big goals today. I hope your life is filled with enthusiasm and high energy from a positive idea. I pray you are driven by the power of a dream.

However, let's put a different spin on that concept today. Let's consider the life-giving phrase: "Believe it and You Will Receive it." God reaches out in love to all of humanity with the most precious gift of all. Yes, God offers the free gift of eternal life to all who believe. God says in John 3:16:

For God so loved the world that He gave His only begotten Son, that whoever believes in Him should not perish but have everlasting life.

Yes, my friend, God loves you today. In fact, He loves you so much He gave His one and only Son to dies on the cross for you. Jesus went to the cross and paid the penalty for our sins. Christ died and rose again in order to offer His free gift of eternal life. Faith in Christ totally erases our sin debt to God.

Faith in the New Testament means two things. First, the acceptance of the facts. That would be the complete confidence that Jesus is the eternal Son of God. Jesus is the one who left heaven and came to this earth. His birth was supernatural and His life was a perfect, completely without sin. He went to the cross and gave His life as an atoning sacrifice for our sins. Jesus died as our substitute as He paid the total price for our sins. He rose again the third day. The resurrection of Christ proves His sacrifice totally satisfied God the Father as a payment for our sins.

I trust you believe the facts of the Gospel concerning the death, burial, and resurrection of Christ. However, that is only step one in saving faith. Next, we must place our trust in Christ as Lord and Savior. This moves our faith from the head to the heart. This often takes our faith from the formal to the personal. We must totally trust Christ and Christ alone for our eternal life.

One of the best illustrations of saving faith is found in the legendary story of Charles Blondin. It seems that in 1858, the daredevil, Charles Blondin, announced he would cross the Niagara Falls on a tightrope. He boldly proclaimed he would walk across the falls on a tightrope using only a 40-pound pole for balance. Charles Blondin was considered the greatest tightrope walker in the world and this would be his most daring venture. The date was scheduled for June 30, 1858.

Well, as you can imagine, the news of Blondin's bold announcement spread like wildfire. Trains began to pour into Toronto, Canada and Buffalo, New York. Thousands of people came to see the predicted excitement over the Niagara Falls.

It would be a daring and dangerous event to say the least. No net would be stretched to protect him if he fell. Should Charles Blondin lose his footing, he would plunge to his death. He was a bold and brazen man willing to risk his life. The excitement of such an event was electrifying the huge crowd that had gathered.

Finally, the big day arrived. The rope was stretched across the falls. Blondin would begin on the Canadian soil and cross over into America. The mighty Niagara River that plunged over the falls would be raging below him.

The crowd watched intently as Blondin began his breath-taking adventure. He began to walk slowly and deliberately on the wire.

One step in front of another as he walked across the powerful falls. He held the 40-pound pole as he carefully kept his balance.

Finally, he reached the other side. The crowd cheered wildly above the roar of the falls. The crowd was ecstatic! The crowd clapped and cheered as Blondin smiled and waved.

Then Blondin stunned the crowed again. He was ready to reach into his bag of tricks and continue to entertain the crowd. Charles Blondin announced he would return back across the falls. He would cross the mighty Niagara again that day and return to Canadian soil.

Then he made a shocking claim. Blondin shouted he would not return alone. He would cross the falls carrying a full-grown man on his back. The crowd went crazy with excitement. Blondin asked the crowd this question - "How many believe I can carry a full-grown man on my back across the falls?" The crowd shouted - "We Believe" - "We Believe" - "We Believe."

Blondin then asked a heart-stopping question. Who will be the man? Silence fell across the crowd. No one would volunteer. They shouted they believed, but were unwilling to trust him. Finally, in desperation, Blondin turned to his manager, Harry Colcord, and asked if he believed Blondin could carry him on his back across the falls. Colcord responded - "I have no doubt at all." Blondin then asked Colcord if he would trust him. Harry Colcord said, "I will."

The crowd watched in disbelief as Harry Colcord climbed onto the back of Charles Blondin. Once again the rope was tightened and Blondin began the dangerous journey carrying Colcord on his back. You could cut the tension of the crowd with a knife. Blondin was doing the impossible and Colcord was believing the incredible.

However, as Blondin reached the halfway point, the event took a dangerous turn for the worse. A gambler cut one of the guide wires and the rope began to sway fearfully back and forth. Blondin stopped and went to his knees clinging to the tight rope. He told Colcord to get off his back. The crowd looked on in horror as the two men dangled over the raging falls.

Blondin looked Colcord in the face and shouted this: "Harry, you are no longer Colcord, you are Blondin. When I sway, you must sway. You must become a part of me or we will both plunge to our death. Now, climb onto my back."

Colcord climbed onto Blondin's back in a death-defying feat. Suddenly, Charles Blondin began to run at full speed. The rope was swaying wildly back and forth as Blondin raced with Colcord on his back. How he kept his balance, no one could understand. The falls thundered below him as he literally ran for his life. It was an act of concentration and balance like no one had ever seen before.

Finally, Blondin safely stepped onto Canadian soil. The people went wild with excitement! It was one of the most incredible death-defying acts in the history of entertainment.

Yes, this amazing story accurately illustrates true faith. Many said they believed Blondin could do it, but only Harry Colcord placed his trust in Charles Blondin. Today, the question is asked. Do you believe Jesus died and rose again for your sins? Many shout back, "We believe, we believe."

However, true faith places your life into the Lord's hands. You must personally trust Him to carry you safely to a real place called heaven. The distractions of the world roar like the powerful Niagara Falls. But make no mistake about it; if you trust in Jesus, then He will carry you to safety. His gift of eternal life is for all who believe. That means to accept the facts of the gospel and totally trust in Jesus Christ as Savior and Lord.

Believe it and you will receive it. Tell God you believe Christ died and rose again for your sins. Then, by faith invite Christ into your life as personal Lord and Savior. My friend, you make a personal decision for Christ and the incredible gift of eternal life will be yours. John 1:12 says, "But as many as received Him, to them He gave the right to become children of God, to those who believe in His name." I trust you will believe it and receive it.

CHAPTER 51

THREE WORDS DESCRIBE CHRISTMAS, "GOD WITH US"

If we could condense all the truth of Christmas into three words, they would be: "God With Us." Matthew 1:23 says:

Behold, the virgin shall be with child, and bear a Son, and they shall call His name Immanuel, which is translated, "God with us."

You see my friend; the Babe in the manger was the sovereign, omnipotent, creator of heaven and earth. Jesus was and forever shall be: "God with us."

Through the person of Christ, God came down to our level. God reached down in Christ in order to lift us up to God. Through the incarnation, God has identified with humanity. He knows how we feel in order to identify with the problems of human frailty. However, because of His deity, God will meet our every need through the person of His Son, Jesus Christ.

I'm reminded of Peter the Great, who learned to identify with the ship builders of his country. Peter the Great was the Tsar of Russia during the early1700's. He was a very powerful and intelligent man occupying the Russian throne. All of Russia was at his beck and call and he usurped his authority in a commanding way.

He was the first Tsar who attempted the blend the ways of Europe with Russia. He attempted to change Russia's way of living. He adopted European styles of dress and made the use of tobacco mandatory among the members of his court. He would even summon the great nobles before him and clip their beards with his own hand. Of course, anyone who would oppose him, he would have put to death for all to see. This even included the execution of his own son. Yes, he was a very powerful man and certainly feared by all.

However, one of the things that intrigued Peter the Great was the ship building industry of England and Holland. Consequently, Peter the Great did a most unusual act as a Tsar. He laid aside his kingly clothing and traveled undercover to England. He dressed as a commoner and took a job in the ship building industry. He learned the secrets of the trade from the ground level. This gave him a tremendous perspective on how to build high quality ships. It also gave him first hand experience concerning the day-to-day problems that ship builders face.

Once he had gained the experience he needed, he returned to Russia and put on his kingly garments. Then he set out to do the task of teaching the Russians how to build outstanding ships. He was a great teacher because of his knowledge and his ability to personally identify with the needs of the workers. He had the wisdom and power of a king, yet he could also identify with the common people. He had lived their experiences and had gained their perspective.

In a way, that is what God has done for us through Jesus Christ. The King of Kings and Lord of Lords took on human form in the person of Jesus Christ. Almighty God identified with humanity through His Son, the Lord Jesus. The creator has identified in a very personal way with His creation. God became a man in the person of Jesus Christ. We call it the incarnation.

The virgin birth of Christ is a foundational truth of the Christian faith. Isaiah prophesied of the virgin birth long before the angel announced it to Mary. Isaiah 7:14 says,

Therefore the Lord himself will give you a sign: Behold the virgin shall conceive and bear a Son, and shall call His name Immanuel.

Isaiah 9:6 went on to say:

For unto us a child is born; unto us a Son is given; and the

government shall be upon His shoulder. And His name will be called Wonderful Counselor, Mighty God, Everlasting Father, Prince of Peace.

Why would this baby called "Immanuel" bear the title of "Mighty God" and "Everlasting Father?" Because as the Scripture says in Matthew 1:23, the name Immanuel means "God With Us."

That, my friend, is the blessed truth of Christmas. God is with us in the person of His Son, the Lord Jesus Christ. That little baby in the manger was the King of Kings and Lord of Lords. Jesus Christ was conceived by the Holy Spirit, born of the Virgin Mary, and took on human form. The Creator made the ultimate identification with His creation.

That's why the Bible says in Hebrews 4:15, speaking of Jesus:

For we do not have a High Priest who cannot sympathize with our weaknesses, but was in all points tempted as we are, yet without sin.

Yes, Jesus Christ can feel what we feel. He understands our needs because He laid aside His kingly garments and became a man. Here is the good news: Because of His humanity, He understands our weaknesses, but because of His deity, He can give us victory over them.

Yes, Jesus has the full power to strengthen us during any situation. That is why the Scripture says in Hebrews 4:16:

Let us therefore come boldly to the throne of grace, that we may obtain mercy and find grace to help in time of need.

Yes, Christ has all the power we need to help us with the problems of life. He laid aside His kingly garments and left heaven and came to this earth. But remember, His name was called "Immanuel" which means "God with us."

That's right, He is the eternal Son of God. He has gone back to the Father and is now seated at the right hand of the Majesty on high.He offers us entrance into the throne room of God. He invites us to come to speak to Him and talk to Him in prayer. He says to speak to Him because He knows how we feel. He can identify with us today.

Have you ever had a problem and needed to talk to a friend who could understand? Jesus Christ offers to be that friend today. He is always available and always has a listening ear for you. Once you have poured out your heart to Him in prayer, He will wrap His loving arms around you and meet your every need. You can lean on His shoulder today.

My friend, Jesus Christ was "God with us" not only to identify with our needs, but also to meet our greatest need. The most important need that we share is the need for forgiveness of sin. That's why Christ came to this earth. The God of heaven laid aside His kingly garments and traveled undercover to the cradle in Bethlehem. You see, the cradle was just the first part of the picture. The next important scene was the cross where Christ gave His life for us.

That's right, Christ was born to die. He humbled Himself and left heaven and went to the cross for our sins. He died and rose again so that we could have a personal relationship with God. Just as Peter the Great left His throne in Russia and went to England and learned the ship building trade, returned to Russia, and taught the people how to build excellent ships, so Christ left His throne, came to this earth and identified with humanity. However, He not only identified with humanity, He sacrificed His life for humanity.

You know, Peter the Great did another unusual act as a king. Once he disguised himself as a beggar and traveled to a village. He went from house to house asking for help. Finally, one man received Him into his home.

The next day, Peter the Great sent the Royal carriage to the man's house. He took the man to Moscow and allowed him to live in the King's Palace. The man had received Peter the Great, and consequently he was treated as royalty.

My friend, Jesus was born in a manger like a common person. The King of Glory arrived in a humble cradle in Bethlehem. Later, He went to the cross and died and rose again for our sins. Today, He knocks on our heart's door and seeks an entrance into our life.

For those who receive Him, Jesus will provide for them for all eternity. He will take you to the Royal Palace of heaven when life is finished on this earth. Yes, the true meaning of Christmas is found in the three words, "God with us."

CHAPTER 52

WITH GOD ALL THINGS ARE POSSIBLE

Some of the most powerful words in all of the Scriptures are found in Matthew 19:26. Jesus said:

With men this is impossible, but with God all things are possible.

Yes, when you put God into any equation, you have the formula for success. God and you always make a majority. The impossible becomes possible with God.

Jesus gave an incredible truth and a foundational principle for success. It is a positive promise based on the unlimited power of God. Burn the thought, "with God all things are possible" deep into your heart and soul. It will give you hope for any situation. Your life will soar to new heights through the power of hope.

You will achieve tremendous accomplishments that you previously considered "impossible." Any obstacle will simply become an opportunity to experience the power of God. A source of energy will empower your life. You will have the faith to set new goals as you look past the moon and reach for the stars.

The words of Philippians 2:13 will come alive in your heart. The Scripture says:

For it is God who works within you both to will and to do of His good pleasure.

This will give you the confidence to climb every mountain. In time, the word "Impossible" will be removed from your vocabulary.

Jesus said it this way in Mark 9:23, "If you can believe, all things are possible to him who believes." Yes, the power of faith will give you a positive focus on life. Remember, your achievement will always begin with your attitude.

Jesus gave us a powerful promise to cling to when He said in Matthew 19:26, "With God all things are possible." Those words have given me a positive motivation and laid the foundation for a positive ministry. I have virtually built my life and ministry on those precious words of Christ.

I remember when I first began to apply the promise, "With God all things are possible," in a very practical way. It was June of 1985, when I first became pastor of what has now become, New Life Baptist Church. We changed to our current name when we relocated our church campus in 1992. Our purpose of the name "New Life" is to identify with our mission. Our goal is to help people discover the "New Life" that Jesus gives through faith in Him.

When I first came to the church, our attendance was very small. In fact, the first Sunday I preached at the church, we had only 23 people in attendance. The church had been in existence for nearly 30 years and had experienced some good times and bad times. It seems that most of the pastors had not stayed very long. In fact, I was the 13th pastor to serve at the church. Quite frankly, in all appearances, it looked like we were facing the "worst of times."

We had an old building that needed some improvements. The drop ceiling in the auditorium was stained from a leaky roof. The dark paneling on the walls and the poor lighting did not exactly give the auditorium a "cheery look." The carpet was very thin from many years of use and needed to be replaced.

The windows in the auditorium were an interesting sight to behold. They were covered with a multi-colored material in an attempt to give a "stained glass" look. However, the material was peeling off and I don't think it resembled stained glass.

My office wasn't exactly plush either. It was an eight-foot by ten-foot baptismal changing room. It had a shower curtain to protect my desk from the splashing water of the baptismal tank. Since my dad was a bricklayer, I was able to solve the problem of no bookshelves. I simply borrowed some concrete blocks and wooden planks and set up my bookshelves. It seemed to enhance my office in some strange way. Most importantly, it helped me identify with the "working man."

Our parking lot also added a unique feature. It was grass! I had never experienced mowing a parking lot until I became pastor of the church. In fact, I don't even remember studying in seminary how to mow the church parking lot. At first, I wasn't sure if I should mow in a square or striped lines, or perhaps cut in a diagonal pattern for "eye appeal."

However, one thing was for sure, it certainly did smell nice at the church. All of the major fast food restaurants were close at hand. Sometimes I would step outside and breath in the mouthwatering aroma of McDonald's, Arby's, Burger King, Taco Bell, and Dunkin Doughnuts. I figured we could possibly attract the "junk food junkies" to the church. They might even enjoy a family picnic on our grassy parking lot. Unfortunately, we soon put in a gravel lot and that eliminated our "picnic outreach."

The church also faced the challenge of very limited financial resources. After all, lack of attendance and lack of funds seem to go hand in hand. The small handful of people did the best they could, but there was just so few of them.

I tell this story for a reason. I know something about facing some overwhelming odds. Humanly speaking, everything was stacked against us. However, "with men this is impossible, but with God all things are possible."

Therefore, the very first thing I did at the church was to have the words "with God all things are possible" printed on our church literature. We printed it on the bulletin, stationary, any type of literature from the church included the positive promise of Jesus. We needed to believe in an all-powerful God. We could not focus on all of the obstacles; we had to focus on the all-powerful God we served.

Fortunately, we had a handful of faithful people who wanted to grow. We believe in the life changing message of the death, burial, and resurrection of Christ. We were committed to sharing the good news of the love of Christ to our community.

We also believe the Bible is the unchanging and eternal Word of the Living God. We believe the entire Bible is the divinely inspired Word of God and is "truth without any mixture of error." II Timothy 3:16 says, "All Scripture is given by inspiration of God, and is profitable for doctrine, for reproof, for correction, for instruction in righteousness."

We also believe in God's promise to bless His Word. Romans 10:17 says, "So then faith comes by hearing, and hearing by the Word of God." I fully believe that the Bible is not a rulebook to make you miserable; it is a roadmap to make you successful.

We have seen God bless His Word time and time again. We have seen hundreds of people come to faith in Christ. We have relocated the church campus and gone through two major building programs. We even met in rented facilities for three and a half years while putting our building program together.

We have seen attendance records as high as 864 for Easter Sunday. Our annual Christmas Pageant has become the highlight of our community during the Christmas Season. We have gone to three performances to accommodate the 1500 plus people that attend each year. All of the participants in the Pageant are volunteers and are members of New Life, yet many have been mistaken as professionals.

God has blessed our Youth and Children's Ministries as well. Young families are excited about bringing their children to church. Our Student Ministry, known as "Real Power", is having a tremendous impact on middle school and high school students. We also run our own youth and children's camp each summer, where many young people strengthen their faith and develop positive friendships.

God continues to open exciting ministry opportunities in our community. We have been given access to the local juvenile center. We have seen many young people who are struggling with difficult problems find their answer to life through faith in Jesus Christ. God has also provided the means for us to establish a Radio Ministry. The Power for Living Broadcast is currently heard on a variety of stations throughout the state.

A few years back, God opened an incredible door for me to serve as team chaplain for a local high school football team. Each week during the season, I lead a volunteer team chapel where 40-50 players attend. It is a tremendous opportunity to spiritually motivate athletes to a standard of excellence to achieve success on and off the field. These are the types of things that people will tell you are impossible, but my friend, "With God all things are possible."

However, it all begins with a personal relationship with God through faith in the Lord Jesus Christ who died and rose again for you. A simple prayer to invite Christ into your life will take your faith from a formal religion to a personal relationship with God. Once you have invited Christ into your life, you will have the confidence to tackle every challenge with the positive faith that *"With God all things are possible"*

For each additional copy, send your $15.00 donation to:

Power for Living Ministry
P.O. Box 4396
South Bend, IN 46634
Email:pflmike@aol.com

Thank you for helping us share the positive faith that believes:
"With God all things are possible"